make the world
a stylish place
AF675067
SEAGRAM'S
BLENDERS
PRIDE
MAGICAL NIGHTS
taste that speaks for itself
Music CDs Experience Seagram's Blenders Pride Magical Nights events.
O&M 5291

vatika Hospitality
passionate.creative.warm
THE BEST OF GURGAON'S FINE DINING EXPERIENCES AT YOUR DOORSTEP.
JING
the FOX
World Cuisine
Coriander Leaf
56
v cater to your style
V
V cater enhances the experience of outdoor catering.
The warmth of hospitality right at your doorstep. Whether it's a cocktail party for 50 friends or a corporate event for 500, beautifully prepared food can appeal to your sense of taste, smell and sight - perhaps even touch.
This is what we intend and deliver with our outdoor food services.
v cater to your style
V
+91 956022266
CALL NOW FOR THE BEST CATERING EXPERIENCE
vcater@vatikagroup.com

TIMES FOOD GUIDE

Chocolates Caterers Tiffin Services
Food Shops Cooking Classes

Delhi Gurgaon Noida Faridabad Ghaziabad

2011

MARRYAM H RESHII

www.timescity.com

Editorial team
Dilip Singh
Chetananand Singh

Design team
Subhasish Munshi
Balkishan Verma
Jitender Kumar

Project editor
Madhulita Mohanty

Marketing team
Rupa Das
Malti Gautam

Production
Neeraj Bharti

Times Food Guide: Delhi

First edition 2011

Published by
Ravi Dhariwal for the proprietors,
Bennett, Coleman & Co. Ltd.,
New Delhi

Times Group Books
(A division of Bennett, Coleman and Company Limited)
Times Annexe, 9-10, Bahadur Shah Zafar Marg, New Delhi-110002

Printed at : Ajanta Offset & Packagings Ltd.

Price: ₹75

CONTENTS

INDICES

AUTHOR'S NOTE

Just a few short years ago, who would have ever thought that a guide like this would have been necessary? If the lady of the house didn't cook, the maid did and that was that. Today with members of a single household strung out over several cities in several states, the old order has changed forever. And that's where our army of caterers, partymakers, bakers and specialist cooks come in. It is no coincidence that many, if not most, of these are specialists in a particular field. A home baker does just that: bakes cakes. A chocolatier supplies only chocolates for the ever burgeoning gifts market in a city once famed for gifting *mithai*. Even the party caterer who has a long line-up of cuisines at hand is a specialist: he has on tap expertise to translate your dreams into reality. Thus, if you want five regional Indian cuisines for your son's wedding, he'll rustle up five of his trusted allies if you want a sit down dinner for your clients where Italian food has to be served, well, that's what he will do with his in-house team.

If you have relocated from elsewhere and cannot be bothered to set up full house in Delhi, yet want the comfort of home cooking, that's available too. Our guide lists not only the largest wedding caterers but the tiniest set-up that specializes in mom's cooking! And if after all that yellow dal and Lauki ki Sabzi, if you want to celebrate your birthday, just call one of our ladies who will whip up a Yuzu Mousse Cake with lavender icing. It's as far as you can possibly get from Mom's baking, unless Mom was trained in the patisserie department of Culinary Institute of America, upstate New York! Just don't try making it at home: you are unlikely to find either yuzu or lavender flowers in your local market: our list of ladies who bake are a fearless lot who hand carry Philadelphia cream cheese in their hand luggage and who make the occasional trip to Paris to pick up their supply of Valrhona Chocolate.

Exhaustive as our list is, we want your help in expanding it. Barrage my inbox with recommendations. I will be happy to check them out. Anonymously of course!

Meanwhile, happy eating. At home, where else!

Marryam H Reshii

ACKNOWLEDGEMENTS

The Times Food & Nightlife Guides are worked upon under the guidance of Vineet Jain, Managing Director, Times Group. His insistence on detail and functionality is what makes the guides so unique and popular. We also thank the following interns for checking and re-checking facts: Ashish Sharma, Deepak Dwivedi and Bhanvi Chaudhary.

HOW TO USE THIS GUIDE

It's simple. It's easy to use. It's been written with you in mind. Your brand-new book has been divided into easy-to-use chapters. Flip to the one which interests you the most. The chapters are…

- Chocolates
- Home Caterers/Professional Home Caterers
- Tiffin Services
- Cooking Classes
- Food Shops & Services

Useful Information: In each chapter, you'll find alphabetical listings with addresses, phone numbers, timings (for some) and clearly marked information. Each one delivers information and gives clear guidelines. Take a look at the horizontal colour bar, in which you will find all the vital details pertaining to each entry. By looking at the strip you'll immediately know what cuisine is on offer, the timings and the rating too. Look for the following information: cuisine, timings and ratings on the basis of food (where applicable).

Let's take a look at:

CHOCOLATES
Even if you do not have the time to read the review, the rating instantly reveals that food is very good at Chocolate Obsessions. The food has been rated at 3.00 (Good). The cuisine is Chocolates and timings are 2pm to 8pm.

HOME CATERERS/PROFESSIONAL HOME CATERERS
Many of those who are featured here work out of home. Some of them do have retail outlet. There, only the Food has been rated. All the cuisines offered by them have been marked clearly though.

Name | Cuisine | Rating | Timing

Chocolate Obsessions
CHOCOLATES
Food- 3.00 | 2pm to 8pm

Vanita Malhotra is a trailblazer of sorts. Two years back she began with home-made tea cakes, choco chip muffins and brownies. Today she is in the thick of chocolate-making. She also takes customized orders for gifting assorted cakes and muffin baskets, all freshly baked at her home. She also takes orders for Western desserts like chilled Souffle, Cheese Cake, Tiramisu, Chocolate Mousse and Apple Pie. Some of her speciality chocolates are Rum Balls Chocolates, Truffles Chocolates with Coffee, Butterscotch Chocolates, Hazelnut Chocolates, Liqueur-filled Chocolates and Chocolate Moulded Flower-shaped lollipops. You need to inform her in advance if you want to place a bulk order. And you also require to deposit part of the payment which could be between 25 and 50 per cent, depending on the value of your order. You can reach Vanita at: *vanita_malhotra@hotmail.com.*

■ **D 004, Park View City I, Sohna Road, Gurgaon,**
Ph: 0124-4015752, 9818503550

Address | Review | Phone No

TIFFIN SERVICES
This is simple, clear and self-explanatory. It lists the healthy Indian lunch providers with details of what all is on offer.

FOOD SHOPS AND SERVICES
Just by studying the colour strip you can get to know that Navdanya is an organic store and requires a minimum order of ₹1,000 and a day's notice for home delivery. But you need to be a member of Navdanya.

COOKING CLASSES
This chapter is self-explanatory again… for instance, Nita Mehta teaches various courses in cooking for which the fee begins from ₹.900/class.

1	**POOR**
1.25	Average – – –
1.50	Average – –
1.75	Average –
2	**AVERAGE**
2.25	Average +
2.50	Average ++
2.75	Average +++
3	**GOOD**
3.25	Good +
3.50	Good ++
3.75	Good +++
4	**VERY GOOD**
4.25	V.Good +
4.50	V.Good ++
4.75	V.Good +++
5	**EXCELLENT**

RATINGS: Here I would like to place on record that the Ratings have been done as objectively as possible. A lot of factors were here taken into consideration... great dishes, ambience, service, style, value-for-money, comfort, luxury... not all of them at the same time and not at all in this order. The most important being consistency. The establishments are rated on Food. All three variables between average and good: average +, average ++ and average +++. Here's some more detail. It's very critical that you look at these Ratings carefully.

REVIEW PARAGRAPH: My idea is to reconstruct the eating out experience for you, as accurately as possible. That's what my review attempts to do. It points out not just the 'must tries' but also the 'must avoids'. The specialities and the ambience too.

TOP CHOICES: Right upfront, check out the 'Pick of the Guide' for the best in each category.

Enjoy using it. Hope it helps in making your life hassle-free and, of course, delicious!

Marryam H Reshii

BEST OF DELHI

BEST OF MUMBAI

BEST CONFECTIONERY SHOPS

Bombay Baking Co
Theobroma
The Gourmet Shoppe & Snack Bar
Desiree — The Cake Studio
Indigo Delicatessen
La Patisserie
Sugar N Spice
Deliciae Desserts, Coffees & More
Gourmet Store
Le 15
Moshe's
Gaylord Bakeshop

BEST CHOCOLATIERS

Fantasie Fine Chocolates
Choc Affaires
Chocossieur
Napoleon Chocolatier
Patchi
Brujin

BEST BROWNIES

Brownie G
Choc Affaires
Cake Line
Sleight of Hand
Indulge

BEST HOME-MADE DESSERTS

Desserts 'R' Us (Winner)
Firoza Moos
Beena Fernandes
Cake Line
Desiree — The Cake Studio
Dolce
Goriawala
Indulge
Shirin Adenwalla
Sugar Rush
Venial Sin
Villie Mehta
Chocolate Is My Religion
Crumbilicious
Parfait

BEST CATERERS

BEST MULTI-CUISINE

Food Link
H.A.S. It All Foods
Moveable Feast
Catering & Allied
Cheron Caterers
Fountain Caterers
Harpal Singh

BEST EUROPEAN/GLOBAL & ITALIAN

Fountain Caterers
Catering & Allied
Peppers – The Home Deli
Shirin Adenwala

BEST MUSLIM & AWADHI

Q's Cuisine
Jeff Caterers

BEST PARSI

Tanaz Godiwalla (Winner)
Zareer Lalkaka
Dalal Enterprises
Abreen Pulao

BEST RAJASTHANI

Satyanarain Maharaj
Kanaklata Institute
SR Foods

BEST CHINESE & ORIENTAL

Mr Chow's
Busaba
Lotus Blossom (Thai)

BEST FOOD SHOPS & SERVICES

CONVENIENCE FOODS

Gomathy Food
Neeta Chawla

NOODLES & WONTON SKINS

Hong Kong Noodles
Suey Quality Products

ORGANIC FOOD

Navdanya
Raja Fun Food Pvt. Ltd.
Naturally Yours

HEALTH SHOP

Health Total
Under the Mango Tree
Eco Corner

GOURMET GIFTS

Brownie G
Desserts 'R' Us
TBZ Nirmal Zaveri
WIT (Women's India Trust)

PICKLES & MASALAS

Konkan Spices/Curry Masala
Mummy's Yummies

READY TO EAT

Fortune Gourmet (imported cold cuts and seafood)
Chenab Impex (olives, etc)
Gogo Snacks (farsaan)
Prakash Chilly (Chilli Relish)

TABLE DÉCOR HOME ACCESSORIES

Good Earth
Contemporary Arts
Frazer & Haws
Jayshree & Tejas Gandhi
Om Visual Crafts & Artifacts

CHOCOLATES

All Time Celebration

CHOCOLATES
Food-2.50

Tanu Garg, the proprietor of All Time Celebration at Noida, has earned quite a reputation making chocolates for nine years. It has to be said that chocolate making initially started out as an adjunct to her main business: trousseau packing. Rock Crunchy and Mint-flavoured Chocolates are what she makes best. The former is her home-created confection of puffed rice, brittle and mixed nuts. She usually supplies bulk orders which you need to give two days to almost a week in advance. You also need to pay 25 per cent of the cost as advance. Wedding invitations, birthdays and corporate gifting are her specialities.

■ 7/408, Silver Estate Apartment, Near Kendriya Vihar, Sector 50, Noida, Ph: 9818697899

Avneet's Dream Creation

CHOCOLATES
Food-2.50

Avneet's Dream Creation makes chocolates for friends, relatives and acquaintances only. The quality of her products has been advertised by word of mouth and she has done well during the three years that she has been in chocolate business. Avneet is capable of handling large volume orders of upto 50kg. But you need to notify her two to 10 days in advance. Almond Chocolates, Vanilla Chocolates, Walnut Chocolates, Strawberry Chocolates and Coconut Chocolates are their specialities. She is essentially a home-based operator whose quality has brought her into the limelight in the neighbourhood. Particularly sought-after for children's birthday return gifts, she customizes shapes for chocolate bonbons. Letters of the alphabet are always a hit.

■ 11B, Pocket A12, Kalkaji Extn, Kalkaji, Delhi, Ph: 9810293932

Belgique

11am to 10pm

CHOCOLATES
Food-2.75

If you wish to gift dark chocolate to someone special there is no better place for you to go to than Belgique. With a wide variety on offer, you will never be disappointed here. All their couverture (raw chocolate) is said to be Belgian. Some of the fillings are liqueur, raisins, fudge, truffles, nuts, marzipan, coconut, and orange. It also has an array of cakes — Dark Chocolates, Malted Chocolates and Dry Fruit Chocolates. Its USP is reasonable price — ₹1000 for one kg.

■ 1st Floor, DT City Centre, Gurgaon, Ph: 9999000894

Blessings

CHOCOLATES
Food-2.75

Blessings owner Kavita Chadha has been making chocolates at her home in Rajinder Nagar. Fruit and Nut Chocolates, Rum and Raisin Chocolates, Hazelnut Chocolates, Truffle

Chocolates, Chocolate Coated Cookies are some of the varieties she makes best. Some of these are soft-centred chocolates and the chocolate is made from imported couverture. During the last five years as a chocolate maker, she has made a fine reputation among customers who include corporates, friends and acquaintances. Baby showers, children's party return gifts and wedding invitations are just some of the occasions she provided chocolates for. She has a range of her own boxes at all price points if required. She can deliver 100-200kg of chocolates at a day's notice, if you are willing to make an advance payment of 50 per cent.

R 783, Rajinder Nagar, New Delhi, Ph: 9810008153, 28742581

Brown Bite

CHOCOLATES
Food-2.50

Sunita Bhasin makes exotic chocolates — Chocolate Truffles, Caramelized Almond Chocolates, Honey and Fig Chocolates as well as Enrobed Chocolates. Enrobed chocolates include those that have not been placed into a mould, but where the fillings (i.e. nut clusters) have been poured over with chocolate. Her Honey and Fig chocolates are moulded and are something of a speciality. Her other speciality is enrobed fruit, especially banana slices and strawberries. Once you have paid 30 per cent of the money in advance you can rest assured that Sunita will deliver the goods on time. But she needs a notice of around three to 10 days, depending upon the quantity you order. She takes bulk orders too. Quite a few reputed corporate houses are her clients.

E 61, 1st Floor, Near Central Market, Lajpat Nagar II, New Delhi, Ph: 9811272138, 41723089

Cafferels

CHOCOLATES
Food- 3.25

Cafferels owner Ritesh Chopra does all kinds of chocolate from plain to almonds, the entire variety of nuts and all the usual soft centre fillings. A complete list of the flavours is available on their website *www.cafferels.com.* As regards shapes, they have a complete range of moulds ranging from the praline variety to the animal figures, various types of hearts, flowers, bottles, cars, diaper pins, baby soothers, three-dimensional figures of bunnies and footballs, etc. They also do edible print chocolates which are made with edible, food-grade, imported transfers and silver and golden spray-painted chocolates. Packaging is a USP: they do baby shower packs with chocolates, and wedding boxes with decorated chocolates coordinated with the invitations. They also custom-print the foil wrappers of the chocolates to display your corporate logo or the event for which the pack is made. They do special return-gift chocolate boxes with each recipient's name printed on it.

A 27F, Sector 16, Noida, Ph: 9811723458

Choc Arena

CHOCOLATES, CAKES — 8am to 8pm
Food-2.75

Sisters-in-law Reema and Preeti have together been making chocolates and cakes without icing in their home for two years now. The cakes are tailored to your order, but typically consist of carrot and walnut, date and walnut, honey and walnut with sugar craft topping. As their cakes are usually delivered in bulk, the shelf life needs to be longer than an iced cake. Conversely, sugar craft needs more skill than simple icing. They can deliver as much as 400kg or even more of chocolates but you need to tell them one week to 10 days in advance. They make different types of chocolates — Liqueur Chocolates, Butterscotch Chocolates, Nut Chocolates, Hazelnut Chocolates, White Chocolates and many more varieties. The dry cakes they make are often used as return gifts on birthdays. If you require bigger cakes you have to inform them at least six days in advance.

■ **E 29, Bali Nagar, New Delhi, Ph: 9891560053, 981086893**

Choco Affairs

CHOCOLATES
Food-2.75

For six years Vandana Mathur has been preparing chocolates at home and catering to orders from corporate houses, travel agencies and tour operators as also for weddings, anniversaries and parties. She takes bulk orders, apart from the small ones which come her way every now and then. Among her select repertoire are Chocolate Crunch, Butterscotch Chocolates, Nut Chocolates, Rum and Raisin Chocolates and Irish Chocolates. As she specializes in children's birthday party return gifts, she has a range of adorably childlike shapes like diaper pins, teddy bears, rocking horse, and other kiddie delights. With an advance payment of 20 per cent and a notice of two days you can expect Vandana Mathur to deliver your order on time.

■ **CA/3A, Near RBI Colony, Shalimar Bagh, New Delhi, Ph: 9891497329, 9350250028**

Choco House

CHOCOLATES 9am to 8pm (Open all days)
Food-2.75

Smriti has been making home-made chocolates for a little more than a year now. She not only sells home-made chocolates but also beautiful gift wraps in which you can give them away on occasions like Diwali, Christmas, birthdays, anniversaries, and weddings, etc. Plain Milk/White/Dark Chocolates, Nutty Marble Chocolates, Honey Almond Blast Chocolates, Chocopie, Choco Rock, and Crackle Chocolates are some of Choco House's specialities. It doesn't matter where you live in Noida . The delivery of your order is guaranteed if you place it in advance. Smriti also teaches the art of making chocolates.

■ **Sector 50, Noida, Ph: 9899924610**

Choco Parks

CHOCOLATES
Food- 2.75

What Ritika Pall loves most is making chocolates for friends and acquaintances. However, she is not at all averse to taking orders from corporate houses. She makes delicious chocolates and some of the varieties she makes at her home in Rajouri Garden are Roasted Almond Chocolates, Crunchy Chocolates and Butterscotch Chocolates. She always has these flavours in stock in her house for on-the-spot purchases.You can place your order with Ritika only if you want 10kg and more. She also takes bulk orders for up to 40 to 50kg. But for that kind of order you need to give her a notice of one week. Ritika's chocolate costs ₹650 per kg and up.

■ **V 239, Rajouri Garden, New Delhi, Ph: 41447461, 9811758300, 9899658300**

Choco Smith

CHOCOLATES
Food-2.75

The chocolates that Choco Smith makes are even better than what their website (*www.chocosmith.com*) promises. Two years ago, a pair of professional chocolate makers got together to open Choco Smith in Saket to sell home-made chocolates. They came up with Honey Nougat Chocolates, Coconut Chocolates, Tangy Orange Chocolates, Caramel Crunch Chocolates, Butterscotch Chocolates, Roasted Cashew Chocolates, Gold Truffle (Rum) Chocolates and many more varieties. They are much in demand on occasions like birthdays and anniversaries, though their forte is corporate gifting, for which they have a range of packaging options. You can order more than 100kg of chocolates but you have to tell them two days in advance and make a 30 per cent down payment. Here you can expect customized chocolates with logos of companies or even names of your loved ones. Choco Smith even gift-wraps them.

■ **A7/3, Opp PVR, SFS Flats, Saket, New Delhi, Ph: 9910143646, 9717881317, 66362835**

Chocoholic

CHOCOLATES
Food-2.50

Meenakshi Kapur usually takes bulk orders for home-made chocolates. Corporate houses figure on her list as does Oceans Hospitality, a fast food eatery chain. In addition, she is called upon to make chocolates for children's birthday party return-gifts, for which dinosaur shapes are her most popular ones. Choco Nut, Fruit and Nut Chocolates, Butterscotch Chocolates, Rum & Raisin Chocolates, Strawberry Chocolates, and Vanilla Chocolates are some of the varieties that you will find at Chocoholic. As with other suppliers, you need to make part of the payment in advance. For the past five years she has been operating from her home.

■ **74, Gujranwala Town II, Delhi, Ph: 9899150221, 27213436**

ChocoHub

CHOCOLATES
Food-2.50

Neelam Arora has been making for about a year now chocolates of all varieties — Butterscotch Chocolates, Chocolate Crunch, Strawberry Chocolates, Almond Chocolates, White Chocolates, Rice Crispies, etc. She takes small and big orders from corporate houses and weddings for which she also has her own range of packaging material. She also caters to people celebrating birthdays, anniversaries, etc. Give Neelam your order two days to one week in advance and make a pre-payment of 30 to 40 per cent.

■ **C 9/9293, Vasant Kunj, New Delhi, Ph: 9650477242, 41767274**

Chocolat

CHOCOLATES 10am to 8pm
Food-2.50

Chocolate has always been Kavita Bhatia's passion. For the last two years, however, chocolate-making is her bread and butter. And the quality of her product is something she is most particular about. She has been making all varieties of chocolates from home in Noida — Dark Chocolates, Plain Chocolates, Dry Fruit Chocolates, Liqueur Chocolates and Chocolate Truffles among others. Kavita's chocolates cost ₹800/kg and above, which she can have delivered at your doorstep anywhere in Delhi if you place order for at least 3kg. A 50 per cent deposit is a must at the time of booking orders and this must be done two days in advance.

■ **B 2/707, Purvanchal Silver City Building 11, Sector 93 A, Express Highway, Noida, Ph: 9873430090**

Chocolate Country

CHOCOLATES
Food-2.50

Sumedha takes all kinds of order that come her way and does justice to them all with equal enthusiasm. She makes chocolates for corporate houses, weddings or any other occasion. Liqueur Chocolates that can be made of whisky, rum or vodka, Almond Rock Chocolates that are enrobed, Fruit and Nut Chocolates, Mint Chocolates, Plain Dark Chocolates and Champagne or Wine Chocolates are what she makes best. A few of these are soft-centred chocolates, particularly those with alcohol in them. If you want to order in bulk you have to let her know four days in advance and make a down payment of 30 per cent. Sumedha began making the 'delicious sin' from the ground floor of her house in Gurgaon eight years ago.

■ **U 25, DLF City III, Gurgaon, Ph: 9899274557**

Chocolate Obsessions

CHOCOLATES 2pm to 8pm
Food- 3.00

Vanita Malhotra is a trailblazer of sorts. Two years back she began with home-made tea cakes, choco chip muffins and brownies. Today she is in the thick of chocolate-making. She also takes customized orders for gifting assorted cakes and muffin baskets, all freshly baked at her home. She also takes orders for Western desserts like chilled Souffle, Cheese Cake, Tiramisu, Chocolate Mousse and Apple Pie. Some of her speciality chocolates are Rum Balls Chocolates, Truffles Chocolates with Coffee, Butterscotch Chocolates, Hazelnut Chocolates, Liqueur-filled Chocolates and Chocolate Moulded Flower-shaped lollipops. You need to inform her in advance if you want to place a bulk order. And you also require to deposit part of the payment which could be between 25 and 50 per cent, depending on the value of your order. You can reach Vanita at: *vanita_malhotra@hotmail.com.*

■ **D 004, Park View City I, Sohna Road, Gurgaon, Ph: 0124-4015752, 9818503550**

Chocolate World

CHOCOLATES — 10am to 10pm
Food-2.50

It was just a couple of years back that Manjeet Kaur started making chocolates in her kitchen. At present, she offers ten flavours — Plain Chocolates, Crunchy Chocolates, Truffle Chocolates, Nuts, Cappuccino, Mint Chocolates, Rum Chocolates, Vodka Chocolates, Coconut and Butterscotch Chocolates — all recommended as gifts and for that perfect dessert when hosting a kids' party at home.

■ 404, Gagan Vihar, 2nd Floor, Delhi, Ph: 22530209, 9312269362

Chocolicious

CHOCOLATES
Food-2.75

Radhika has for long been in the business of home-made chocolates. No wonder she has a regular flow of customers who keep flooding her with orders from the small (10kg) to the large (above 100kg). Among her specialities are Truffle Chocolates, Rum and Raisin Chocolates, Nut Chocolates and Flavoured Chocolates. Radhika works with enrobed as well as moulded chocolates. She specializes in wedding-related orders, including baby showers. While she requires two to three days' notice in case of non-bulk quantities, she needs a week to deliver large quantities. An advance payment of 20 per cent is a must.

■ Mayapuri, New Delhi, 9871037579, 9810017209

Choconut

CHOCOLATES
Food-2.50

Choconut began making chocolates a few months back and the clients — mostly friends, acquaintances and relatives — happen to be people from South Delhi area like CR Park, Kalkaji, Greater Kailash, and Pamposh Enclave. They cater to orders of 20kg or more, depending on your order. You can try out Hazelnut Chocolates, Blueberry Chocolates, Rum Truffle Chocolates, Orange Truffle Chocolates, and Dry Fruits Chocolates among the many varieties they have on offer. You need to give a notice of three days and a 30 per cent advance.

■ B 178, Chittaranjan Park, Kalkaji, Delhi, Ph: 9971260604, 9891353391

Coco Ka

CHOCOLATES, BROWNIES, CAKES
Food-2.75

Friends Shikha and Reshma have been making chocolates at their home in Saket in South Delhi. Their business includes everything from single cake orders to substantial orders by corporate houses as well as everything in between. Shikha and Reshma specialize in Liqueur Chocolates, Truffle Chocolates, Centre-filled Chocolates as well as soft-centre chocolates. In addition, they do two types of Cheesecake: baked ones with real Philadelphia Cheese in the New York style as well as chilled Cheesecakes with fruit flavours like strawberry and lemon. Other products are Apple Pies and Brownies. The latter can be made with superior Belgian Chocolate or regular Milk Chocolate. With three days' notice and an advance payment of 50 per cent, you can expect as much as 100kg of any of Coco Ka stuff.

■ **K Block, 8G, Saket, New Delhi, Ph: 9810552188, 9810226535**

Coco Magic

CHOCOLATES
Food-2.75

Hema put her heart into making chocolates five years ago, and quality is something she has never compromised with. This is what makes her popular with clients who always turn to her for both small and bulk orders. Hema makes chocolates for corporate houses, individuals, friends and acquaintances. Assorted Chocolates, Crunchy Chocolates, Fruit & Nut Chocolates, Roasted Chocolates and Butterscotch Chocolates are some of the varieties she does well in. For serving a bulk order she needs three to five days' notice and an advance payment of 30 per cent.

■ **B 9/6413, Vasant Kunj, New Delhi, Ph: 9810711199**

Creative Edge

CHOCOLATES
Food-3.00

Rekha Ghosh has been in the business of making chocolates for over a decade now. She first learnt her craft from a Swiss chocolatier who was impressed with her passion and enthusiasm. Rekha keeps her business niche. Liqueur-filled chocolates like Crème de Menthe and Tia Maria, hard-filling chocolates like nut clusters and superior fruit pulp fillings that nobody else in the home-catering sector seems to be doing are her specialities. Her forte is catering to corporate gifting. She takes great care to ensure that her chocolates are consumed within a couple of weeks of being made.

■ **675, Pocket B, Sector A, Vasant Kunj, New Delhi, Ph: 9810025275**

Deliche

CHOCOLATES
Food-2.75

10am to 8pm

For Priyanka chocolate was once a passion but it has now been her profession for the last five years. No wonder she has stretched herself a little beyond making Brownies, Chocolate Fudge, Molten Lava Cup Cakes, Blueberry Cakes, Chocolate Nougat Cakes, etc. Her USP is the quality of her products — something she has never compromised on. Priyanka usually makes Milk, Dark and Bitter Chocolates. Some of the specialties at Deliche are Truffle Chocolates, Liqueur Chocolates — Whisky, Rum and Brandy — Mint Chocolates, Coffee Truffle Chocolates, Butterscotch Chocolates, Hazelnut Chocolates, Orange Chocolates, and Chocolate Noughat Truffle. For her clients she also packs her chocolates in boxes. She receives corporate orders apart from bookings for anniversaries, weddings and birthday parties. She can deliver upto 500 kg of any of her fare against 50 per cent advance payment and one week's notice.

■ 15/8, FF, Kalkaji, New Delhi, Ph: 9810223203

Designer Home-made Chocolates

CHOCOLATES
Food- 2.75 | Cost: ₹600/kg

Disha Mahajan is a chocolate-maker with a difference. She is not content with just making all kinds of chocolates. She even designs them and gives lesson in the art of making them. A visit to her home, where she works, will give you an idea as to how innovative she is with designing chocolates. Hazelnut Chocolates, Tequila Chocolates, Green Tea White Chocolates, Spicy Chocolates and Strawberry Chocolates are some of the varieties that Disha takes delight in making. One kg of chocolates is priced at ₹600. Three-dimensional Rose Chocolates are priced at ₹50 a piece. You need to pay 25 to 50 per cent of the total money in advance with your order. For a 10kg order you get free home delivery. For bulk orders she needs to be informed at least a fortnight in advance. Disha has been in this profession for the last three years.

■ A 411, Sarita Vihar, New Delhi, Ph: 9873382111

Disha's

CHOCOLATES — 9am to 10pm
Food-2.75

Prabhat Gupta has been making chocolates for six years now. His firm, Disha's, uses imported chocolates with no preservative at all. Nut Chocolates, Fresh Fruit Filling Chocolates, Rum Chocolates, Mint Chocolates and Truffle Chocolates are some of the varieties that you can ask for here. Fresh Fruit Filling requires a fair amount of skill to ensure that the fruit does not spoil and usually includes seasonal fruit: mango in summer, orange in winter and banana through most of the year. Disha's also makes Choco Cookies and they can deliver up to 10 to 20 kg of them. You can order as much as 500kg of chocolates or even more but you have to place advance order. They make 12 to15 varieties of chocolates.

■ 21/4727, Daryaganj, New Delhi, Ph: 9810131570, 9312681070, 9810639325

Good Factory

CHOCOLATES
Food-2.50

Janhvi Bhasin owns the Good Factory which manufactures delicious chocolates which all of us love to eat. Crunchy Chocolates, Nut Chocolates, Mint Chocolates, Rum and Raisin Chocolates and flavoured chocolates — you will get them all at Good Factory. Janhvi has been in the business for a year and takes only small orders — less than 5kg. She fondly remembers the engagement ceremony she supplied chocolates for: both the box and the chocolates were in the shape of rings. Mostly friends, acquaintances and individuals book their orders on occasions like birthdays, weddings, anniversaries, etc. A pre-payment of 40 per cent and two days of notice is needed to book orders here.

■ 36/5, Near Siddhartha Hotel, East Patel Nagar, New Delhi, Ph: 9899002618

I'm Special (Arsh Creation)

CHOCOLATES
Food-2.75

For three years Kavita Khanna has been preparing handmade chocolates at Lajpat Nagar. She is comfortable taking orders of 50kg and less. I'm Special makes Almond Chocolates, Truffle Chocolates, Walnut Chocolates and Mint Chocolates for corporate houses and for people celebrating occasions like birthdays, weddings and anniversaries. Just pay her an advance of 50 per cent and give her two days' notice.

■ **B 7, 2nd Floor, Lajpat Nagar, Part III, New Delhi, Ph: 66217155**

Indulgence

CHOCOLATES
Food-2.50

What was a hobby for Anuradha turned into a full-fledged business after much coaxing by family and friends. A young mother and a dental surgeon by profession, she is a stickler for quality. Cooking has been a passion for her but when her son asked for chocolates almost daily she thought of making them at home and adding some nutritional value to them as well. Her repertoire includes Fruit and Nut Chocolates, Soft-Centred Mint Chocolates, Strawberry Chocolates, Almond Rocks in various shapes like teddy bear, and rabbit. For adults, there are Liqueur Chocolates, Rum Truffle Chocolates, Rum 'n' Raisin among others. Contact her for customized chocolates which are great for birthday parties, anniversaries, weddings or for those from corporate houses. Call her two to three days in advance to book your order with her. Find out more about her at *www.indulgence.co.in.*

■ **Model Town, Delhi, Ph: 9868414455, 9868088604**

Madhu's Bakery

CONFECTIONER/CHOCOLATIER
Food-2.50

Madhu Suri, the lady behind Madhu's Bakery, makes cakes, cookies and chocolates. She has been in this business for a little more than two years. Chocolate Truffle Cake, Strawberry Mousse as well as other fruit-flavoured mousse cakes are some of the specialities she does. Other products include Biscuits enrobed with Chocolate, Crunchy Chocolates, Almond Chocolates and Nutty Chocolates. They mostly cater to friends and acquaintances but you too can place an order. Madhu can deliver upto 4kg of chocolates or bakery stuff at three days' notice and against advance payment.

■ **2nd Floor, W 104, Near Archana Complex, Greater Kailash, New Delhi, Ph: 9958301195**

Mithaimate.com

CHOCOLATES, CAKES, COOKIES, BROWINES, MITHAI — 9am to 7pm
Food- 3.00

Mithaimate.com owner Akhilesh Bali is based in Delhi but promises to deliver chocolates, cakes, cookies, brownies, *mithai* and sugarfree gifts not only in the Captial city but anywhere in India. Within two to three days you will get their products even if you are located in far-flung North-eastern region of the country. And 24 hours is enough for delivery within Delhi and the NCR. Mysore Pak Special, Mathura Peda, Kaju Katli are some of mithais in the bestseller category. Mithaimate.com makes 60 to 70 varieties of chocolates of different shapes and sizes. From the bakery gifts section you can opt for Oreo Brownie, Mocha Chocolates, Honey Nut Brownies, Dark Sinful Chocolate Brownie, Mars Mania and Blueberry Cheesecake packed in gift boxes. Those who have to take care of your sugar level, sugarfree Beda Halwa and sugarfree Nutkhut are worth trying out. Visit Akhilesh's wesite www.mithaimate.com for details of the varieties, their rates and how to order online. Write to akhilesh.bali@mithaimate.com to place your order.

■ **Ph: 65027671, 9818300391**

Megha Chocolate

CHOCOLATES
Food-2.50

From her home in Kalkaji, Megha makes chocolates as well as takes classes on chocolate-making. Almond Chocolates, Vodka Chocolates, Caramel Chocolates, Cream Chocolates, Coffee Chocolates, Cashew Chocolates, Butterscotch Chocolates, Liqueur Chocolates, Pistachio Centre Chocolates and Mango Centre Chocolates are the varieties she makes well. One kg of her chocolates costs ₹600. Give her a few days' notice while placing your order. She will also expect a down payment of 25 per cent if you need 10 kg or more. Megha has been making chocolates for about a year now.

■ **C 99 A, 2nd Floor, Near JEMS College, Nehru Place, Kalkaji, New Delhi, Ph: 9999438543, 9278607650**

Melt O Choc

CHOCOLATES
Food-2.50

Melt O Choc, in this business for five years now, makes chocolates for government offices and friends and acquaintances mostly. Some of their specialties are Walnut Chocolates, Assorted Chocolates and Liqueur Choc — Cocktail and Rum. The lady behind this venture insists that her blend of cocktail is very different from that offered by other players. For bulk orders Melt O Choc requires four days' notice and an advance payment of 50 per cent. Melt O Choc also does a small range of cakes, of which two are carrot cake and Chocolate Truffle.

■ **15, 1st Floor, Near Metro Station, Panchkuian Road, Connaught Place, New Delhi, Ph: 9958070454, 9871030418**

Mini's Home Baked Cake

CAKES, CUP CAKES
Food-3.00 | Cost: ₹300/kg

For 17 years Mini's Home Baked Cake has been catering to the people of Vasant Kunj. They make tea cakes and cup cakes as well as breakfast bakery like croissants and Danish. Walnut cakes, date cakes and brownies are specialities you can try out. This is a very personalized service where each cake is baked with passion. Only pure butter is used and cakes for children are commonly ordered from here. One kg of cake costs ₹300/kg and 1kg is the minimum quantity that she takes order for. You need to inform Mini's Home Baked Cake a day in advance about your order. If you have to order in bulk you need to pay in advance. You can get your stuff delivered at home if you live within a 5km radius.

■ **Vasant Kunj, New Delhi, Ph: 26899365**

Neeti's Home-Made Chocolates

CHOCOLATES
Food-2.75

Neeti's Home-Made Chocolates has been supplying chocolates to corporates clients, friends and acquaintances. Wedding orders are her speciality. Among the over 25 varieties of chocolates that Neeti makes are Crunchy Chocolates, Almond & Walnut Chocolates, Liqueur, Cappuccino and many more. Her most unusual shape is a three-dimensional rose. On a notice of two days to one week, Neeti's can deliver as much as 100kg of chocolates.

■ 03, Opp. Panchsheel Club, Sarvapriya Apartment, Sarvapriya Vihar, Panchsheel Park, New Delhi, Ph: 9871126565, 26520403

Patchi

CHOCOLATES 10.30am to 8.30pm
Food-2.75

This is a chocolate giant from Lebanon, but compared to chocolates from the Western world, Patchi just doesn't cut the mustard. The chocolates are not dark, but extremely sweet and milky. Still, they must be catering to some tastes! On the plus side, the chocolates are wrapped mainly in matte-finished gold paper and look festive in a gift hamper. On the minus side, ₹3,500-₹3,800 can get you a far higher quality of imported chocolates elsewhere. They also have lower priced options of a too-sweet nougat in cellophane wrapping, sweet-sour nougat candy and packaged dragees. Their best chocolate is a real date enrobed with chocolate.

■ Shop No. 13 A, Ground Floor, Select City Walk, Saket, New Delhi, Ph: 40575038-9

Razzle Chocolates

CHOCOLATES
Food-2.50

Saurabh, the proprietor of Razzle, caters to a wide range of orders for chocolates, from 250 grams to upwards of 100 kg. But a 24-hour notice is a must. While they do a large variety of fillings, their most popular ones continue to be Fruit and Nut Chocolates, and Plain Chocolates. Razzle only deals in milk chocolates, not in dark chocolates. Your order will be made at their workshop and sent to you by courier, whether it is less than a kilogram or more than 100kg, which is why so few customers come with small orders. Pay at least 30 per cent when you book your order. Razzle has been manufacturing chocolates for three years now.

■ D 219, Near Deen Dayal Upadhyaya College, Karampura, New Delhi, Ph: 66264274, 9953168640

Soul Chocolates

CHOCOLATES
Food-2.50

A large clientele and 10 years of business have given Sonia Gupta the confidence to make as many kilos of chocolates as any customer might want. Usually, Soul Chocolates are a hit with corporates who give most of bulk orders but they also cater to families and individuals. What Soul does best is Roasted Almond Chocolates, Truffle Chocolates, Liqueur

Chocolates, Nut Chocolates, etc. They need a notice of two days and an advance payment of at least 20 per cent.

Ist Floor, L 13/6, DLF Phase II, Near Sherwood, Gurgaon, Ph: 66227163

Srijan

Chocolates
Food-2.50

You get all kinds of flavoured chocolates at Srijan. That apart, Choco Praline, Almond Chocolates, Truffle Chocolates, Butterscotch Chocolates, Caramel Chocolates, Rum and Raisin Chocolates, Mixing Chocolates, etc. are all available. A Mixing Chocolate refers, in their parlance, to two or more flavours that are combined together. Srijan mostly makes these delicious savouries for corporate houses and for occasions like anniversaries, birthdays, and weddings. They have been in the business for just two-and-a-half years but have earned a place for themselves. A 50 per cent advance and three days' notice must come with every order. Even if you need 200kg, Srijan will not disappoint you.

PP 104, Pitampura, New Delhi, Ph: 9871355347, 9999266344

Sweets And Bitters

Chocolates
Food-2.75

You may have encountered Ritu Gupta's chocolates without realizing it: she retails in a host of fairs and exhibitions throughout the winter months that are held by NGOs, and many of her regular customers visit here at these times to stock up on her products. Having been in the business for over 15 years, she has a keen sense of market trends. Approximately half her clients are expatriates, and her range of shapes for Christmas — bells, Christmas trees, Santa Claus etc. are some of the best in the city. She does Flavoured Chocolates, Liqueur Cocolates and chocolates with soft centres. Her speciality is square boxes and heart shaped boxes with removable lids that you can use to put in a ring. She also does three-dimensional bouquets of roses. There is an address in Sarvodaya Enclave that she can deliver your order to, in the event that her own address in Gurgaon does not suit your convenience.

R 21 B Windsor Court, DLF City Phase IV, Gurgaon, Ph: 9811050960

Tania Arora

Chocolates
Food-2.50

Among the home chocolate-makers, Tania is both enterprising and innovative. Apart from the regular varieties of chocolates, she supplies what she calls designer chocolates — large-sized representations of the Taj Mahal or life-sized wine bottle shapes made out of chocolate. Valentine's Chocolates and above all Paan-flavoured Chocolates are other specialities. In addition, she makes cake pops: a novel cross between a lollipop, a cake and chocolate on a stick. Each is creatively decorated and makes a great gift or party dessert. Her clients are mostly corporate houses who flood her with bulk orders. She also makes chocolates for anniversaries, weddings, birthday parties and for regular clients of course. An advance payment of 50 per cent and two to three days of notice are needed by Tania to service your order. She also packages chocolates in designer boxes.

■ **FB 10, Shivaji Enclave, Rajouri Garden, Delhi, Ph: 9899624707**

Tint N Shade, The Art World

CHOCOLATES
Food- 2.75 | Cost: ₹350/kg

Anjali has bee making chocolates from her Noida home for 10 years now. Rum & Raisin Chocolates, Mint Chocolates, Nuts Orange Chocolates, Almond Chocolates, and Caramel Chocolates are some of the varieties that she makes. Her chocolates cost between ₹350 and 650 per/kg. Be it a birthday party, anniversary or wedding she makes chocolates for all occasions. For an order of 5kg and above one week of notice is required. A deposit of 50 per cent of the total money is also mandatory for placing your order. You can also pay through credit cards. If you live within 12km from her home you can enjoy free home delivery on bulk orders.

■ **C 1/82, Sector 31, Noida, Ph: 0120-2457854, 9810600067**

VC's

CHOCOLATES
Food-2.75

Varsha Choudhary, the proprietor of VC's, has been in the business of producing chocolates, pies, tarts and cakes for four years. Her USP is that none of her range of products contain eggs at all. She makes them for corporate houses, people celebrating anniversaries, birthday parties and for friends and acquaintances. Varsha does Chocolate Truffle, Liqueur Chocolates with whisky, rum or vodka, Fruit Chocolates with fruit in season (orange segments, strawberries or mangoes), Juice Chocolates in which the fillings are almost liquid, etc. One of her virtues is that she never compromises on the quality of her ingredients. She can take an order for 700 kg of chocolate, but you have to tell her a day in advance and pay 30 per cent of the cost while placing order.

■ **E 4, 1st Floor, Opp. Savitri Cinema, GK Enclave Part II, Greater Kailash, New Delhi, Ph: 66264169, 9811422258**

HOME CATERERS

Ahad Sons

NORTH INDIAN (Kashmiri) 10am to 10pm
Food-2.75 | Meal for 2-₹700

Ahad Sons is for lovers of the overwhelmingly meaty Kashmiri cuisine. The three Waza brothers from Kashmir provide party catering and takeaways from their central kitchen. Convenient for when you want to stock up at home. Rista, Gushtaba, Tabak Maz, Rogan Josh and Seekh Kebab are good and authentic. Tomato Paneer, Palak Rista and Haaq are the vegetarian options. However, people are attracted here mainly for the non-vegetarian component. You may resort to Ahad Sons when you have guests over, but they don't do home delivery unless your order is for more than ₹1000. They also offer Gushtabas and Methi Maaz in cans so that you may relish them even months later in some far corner of the globe.

■ **3A, Masjid Moth Village, Uday Park, New Delhi, Ph: 26253642, 26256017**

Ambrosia

MULTI-CUISINE (Italian, Lebanese, Thai, European), **CONFECTIONERY** 9am to 9pm
Food-3.75 | Meal per plate-₹400

The food catered by Ritu Gupta at Ambrosia is Thai, Lebanese and Western. Perfect for a largish dinner, her menu comprises lasagne, pastas, quiches, salads and Lebanese Mezze. Apart from starters and main courses, Ritu also does desserts for which she is deservedly famous. Among the desserts, the house signature is the Ice Cream Cake, of which she always has a few extra in the deep freeze. Other desserts include iced cakes, cheesecakes and tea-cakes like Apple and Prune or Lemon Teacake. She also does a Cointreau Cake, Fresh Fruit Pie, Chocolate Dessert and Bailey's Cheese Cake. Ritu Gupta's desserts are so well-known that several caterers take them for their banquets, so it is possible that you may have tasted her goodies entirely unknowingly. She is popular for her variety of cuisine for which she requires a two-day notice and a minimum order of 10 persons. For desserts, 1 kg is the minimum order and one day's notice is sufficient.

■ **56 A/1, Friends Colony (East), New Delhi, Ph: 26311538, 26842917, 9810088626**

American Ambrosia

CONFECTIONERY 8am to 7pm
Food-2.75 | Meal per dozen-₹500

Uni Vaid occupies a unique place among the home caterers of Delhi. Having lived for a number of years in the USA and specialized in baking, she is somewhat of a specialist in classic American treats like New York Cheese Cake, chewy Fudgy Brownies, Cup Cakes, Bagels and Cinnamon Buns. Among the other things she makes is an American style of baklava, much more flavourful than the Middle Eastern original and Pretzels. She is justly famous for her bagels, which come in six different toppings and are as good as the New York version. Visit her website for details and even placing an order. She does not deliver but your orders must be picked up from her residence. Just remember to order twenty hours in advance, with a minimum order of 12 pieces of cupcakes or bagels.

■ **Ph: 9818433448**

Amrita Kataria

Confectionery 11am to 8pm

Food-3.00 | Meal per plate-₹300

Amrita Kataria is a gifted baker with an artistic imagination. Cakes and desserts are her forte. She can whip up some rather good cheesecakes, Lemon Tarts, brownies and Chocolate Cakes. The Walnut Pie and Chocolates are also recommended. With freshness that you aren't likely to find even at some of the better up-market patisseries in town, Amrita Kataria is an option for those with a sweet tooth. With an extensive menu, you'd think that she would be busy making a whole range of goodies, but her constant grouse is that none of her clients ever want to go beyond her signature Chocolate Truffle Cake! The nicest part of a dessert by this lady is that every stage of the process is done by her alone, guaranteeing a certain quality.

■ **60, Ring Road, Lajpat Nagar, New Delhi, Ph: 29840178, 9811024412**

Aparna and Sulekha Pasricha

Confectionery 10am to 9pm

Food-3.00 | Meal per plate-₹650

Aparna and Sulekha Pasricha are a pair of sisters-in-law who have made a name for themselves in the cake kingdom. Doing what they enjoy most, they have made a profession out of a hobby — just desserts. They take orders for parties and other functions and offer various kinds of cakes, brownies, pies, soufflés, mousses and chocolates. Their speciality is their Ferrero Rocher Cake, Rich Dark Chocolate Cake, Chocolate Truffle, Chocolate Terrine, Almond Nougat Cake and Blueberry Cheesecake and, yes, they also do eggless cakes on request. Some of their teacakes have catapulted them into the big league: Walnut and Date cake with Toffee Sauce for instance. Sugar paste flowers is their speciality and they also do chocolates. Do remember, a minimum order of a 1kg cake and 24 hours notice is required.

■ **C 5/42, Safdarjung Development Area, New Delhi, Ph: 26960150, 26964133, 9810269760**

Arshi Dhupia

Confectionery 9am to 9pm

Food-3.50 | Meal per plate-₹650

Chocolate cravings are what Arshi Dhupia caters to under the banner of 'Cravings'. A confirmed chocoholic herself, it's little wonder that her Rich Chocolate Cakes are her hottest selling product. The Chocolate Truffles, Irish Bailey's Cake and Brownie Cake that Arshi does, all tastefully decorated with sugar flowers and silver leaf, are recommended both as a gift and as for a perfect dessert when hosting a party at home. Also feast on her chilled Cheese Cakes, Irish Dairy Cake, Lemon Cheesecake and the baked New York Cheesecake, Passionfruit with Mascarpone Cake. Give her a 24-hour notice and a minimum order of 1kg. Arshi also does quiches, but those are when she gets time off from her main business — cakes and desserts of the chocolate kind.

■ **100, Golf Links, New Delhi, Ph: 9811296858**

Arvind

MULTI-CUISINE (Thai, Chinese, Indian, European) 9am to 10pm
Food-3.25 | Meal per plate-₹350

Arvind Singh is fiercely reputed for catering to small parties. Try the Chicken Red Curry, Whole Fish with Chilli Sauce or the Stuffed Chicken Wings. Though his speciality is Thai food, Singh has recently begun experimenting with Moroccan and Hyderabadi cuisine as well. But it's the Thai which is guaranteed to get you high! As he has been in the business for a number of years, he has a set formula which has proven to work best. You need to visit his website and choose a menu, and then book it online or over the phone. Depending on the number of guests, one or two delivery boys will arrive at your house at the appointed time with ingredients and cooked dishes. At the speed of lightning, they will assemble the dishes and finish them in your kitchen with the least possible inconvenience to you. A minimum order for 10 persons and two days' advance notice is what he requires. Visit him at *www.arvindji.com*

1A, Maharani Bagh, New Delhi, Ph: 9810145042

Bon Appetit

MULTI-CUISINE (Pure vegetarian Marwari) 9am to 9pm
Food- 3.75 | Meal per plate-₹400

Priti Goenka is the person to turn to for pure vegetarian fare, especially Marwari and Rajasthani dishes like Dal Ki Puri, Sangar Subzi and Gatte Ka Saag. Even though she does provide European and Tex-Mex dishes, it's really her Indian repertoire that she is better known for. Particularly popular is her Mattar Khasta Kachori, which is somewhat of a house speciality. You could try Kolkata Aloo Dum and Dahi/Kanji Vada. Her Badam Seera and Kolkata Gur Sandesh are two of her highly recommended sweet dishes that she does with the quality of a seasoned expert. While most of her food consists of main courses and starters, she does do snacks that you can keep in your house for months. All the food has to be picked up from the Okhla address. Just remember to order 24 hours in advance, with a minimum order of 10 persons.

D 9/3, Okhla Industrial Area, Phase II, New Delhi, Ph: 9810052294, 9811609334

Chitra's Kitchen

INDIAN (Bengali, Anglo Indian, Bengali Muslim) 9am to 5pm
Food-3.75 | Meal per plate-₹600

Chitra Ghose has been in the business of catering for so many decades that she is widely acknowledged to serve the best Bengali meal you will get in Delhi. From Shukhto and Ilish Bhapa to Prawn Malai Curry and Kosha Mangsho, Chitra Ghose's catering — primarily authentic Bengali cuisine — is one of the best things to have happened to Delhi. The scope of her work has increased exponentially over the years, so that it now includes waiters, cutlery, crockery and vessels. As comfortable catering for a party of twenty persons as for a giant wedding for 1,000, Chitra's Kitchen has expanded recently to represent the food of Bengal at hotel food festivals both within the country and overseas. Just be sure to give her a two-day notice, and a minimum order for 10 persons.

C 87, Greater Kailash I, New Delhi, Ph: 9810678663, 9810639720

Desireé

Confectionery 9am to 6pm
Food-2.75 | Meal per plate-₹350

Rebecca Dogra and her daughters are artists in the making. Sugar craft is their forte, and when you see life-like lilies adorning your cake, you will understand the pride they take in their work. They pride themselves for the touch of creativity they add to their cakes. And, indeed, the life-like flowers light up even the most ordinary Chocolate, Plum and Sponge Cakes. Also worth a shot are the Butter Cookies they do. Chocolates, short bread, brownies, marzipan figures and wedding cakes are some of the other goodies on the list. A four-day notice and a minimum order of a 1kg cake is required if you plan to order from here.

■ **78 Galleria, Gurgaon, Ph: 26569965, 26569149, 9818162787, 9910184484**

Foodaholics

Cakes, Mexican
Food-3.75 | Cost of 1 kg cake-₹1500

Reputed to be one of the finest home caterers in the city, Kishi Arora of Foodaholics is first and foremost a baker and patisserie who has studied the craft at the Culinary Institute of America. All key ingredients are supposed to be the finest and brought in by an army of family members and friends. It's only Valrhona Chocolate or Philadelphia cream cheese which she uses. Lavender and yuzu are some of the other flavours that nobody else in the city uses, says Kishi. Don't go to Foodaholics when all you want is a Pineapple Cake! It is only when you are looking for something innovative and aren't quite sure what, that you should give her a try. She also does vegetarian Mexican food that is a lot better than what you get at the so-called Mexican restaurants in the city. And why not! Kishi has lived in Mexico and so knows what its cuisine is really like. Log on to *www.foodaholics.in* to know more about Foodaholics. Send email at: mail@foodaholics.in. You can also place your order on either Facebook or Twitter.

■ **Ph: 9873164293**

Gunjan Goela

Indian 9am to 8pm
Food-3.25 | Meal per plate-₹500

For those looking for an authentic offering of Jain-Marwari food, especially typical of Old Delhi, Gunjan Goela is a one-stop shop. Not only a competent cook herself, she has the uncanny knack of putting various maharajs together by identifying who's the best at what. So for Khurchan, she will get the best Chandni Chowk *halwai,* for Nagori Halwa she'll source the finest for you and for Bedmi Aloo get yet another expert. Same for Daulat ki Chaat, Til Wali Kulfi.... She can also arrange full-fledged meals for *sajan-goaths* and the like. All you have to do is call her and she will organize everything for you. No wonder that she has put together the food for many a Marwari *shaadi.* Just remember to order three days in advance, with a minimum order of 50.

■ **Cottage 3, Oberoi Apartments, Sham Nath Marg, New Delhi, Ph: 9811349055, 9212035323**

Herb Garden

ITALIAN
Food- 3.00

The two *fauji* sisters running this catering service specialize in low-calorie salads and freshly-made pastas. They have a counter in the DLF Promenade Mall which really is a good advertisement for their thriving catering business. They supply office lunches, cater for parties, sell takeaways and serve as the occasional 'pop-up restaurant'. The sisters are sailing along because of their sheer appeal. The best part is that if you specify your favourite ingredients they will create a salad or a hot pasta dish around it. Their salads are imaginative, tasty, fresh and healthy.

▪ 504/40, Heritage City, Next to MGF Metropolitan Mall, MG Road, Gurgaon, Ph: 9810384284

Iram

HYDERABADI 10am to 9pm
Food-3.75 | Meal per plate-400

One of the few Hyderabadi catering businesses in town, Iram has the best food in its category all over the NCR. They make Shikampuri Kebab, with hung curd and onions as a filling in this minced lamb kebab. Other things to watch out for include Chicken Korma, Dum ke Pasande and a superlative, light-as-air biryani and Mirchi ka Salan and Khatti Dal. They only do their trademark Haleem if the order is a minimum of 2kg. Delivery is by the Iram car, for which you pay ₹100 for Gurgaon and ₹300 to South and Central Delhi. The utensils are picked upthe next day.

▪ South City, Gurgaon, Ph: 9811224451

Jaya Kochhar

CONFECTIONERY 9am to 7pm
Food-2.75 | Meal per plate-₹300

Jaya Kochhar is one of the better cake makers in Delhi who operates out of home. She has trained in pastry from Culinary Institute of America, San Fransisco. Her work has a certain class and she is the happiest creating new, out-of-the-box ideas for clients, no matter how painstaking they are. All she needs is a 24-hour notice and a minimum order of a 1kg cake and she can whip up a mean Devil's Chocolate for you. Iced with a thick, sinful layer of marzipan and coloured beautifully, her ultra rich cakes are sinful. With a loyal band of customers, she's a good bet for chocoholics. Her Devil's Chocolate Cake is pretty good, as are her Fudge Brownies, Oatmeal Cookies, Choco Chip Cookies and Lemon Mousse. With marzipan thrown in for good measure, this one is a sugary delight.

▪ A 1/278, Safdarjung Enclave, New Delhi, Ph: 26100729, 9818077161

Jiggs Kalra Catering

MULTI-CUISINE (Indian, European, Italian, Pan-Asian) 9am to 6pm
Food- 3.25

No other caterer in Delhi has perhaps served so many and such celebrities as Jiggs Kalra. You name them and they all have savoured delicacies prepared by his deft and delicate hands: Princess Diana, Pervez Mussharraf, Bill Clinton, Indian presidents and prime ministers. With more than 50 years' experience, the legendary Jiggs' repertoire is as vast as an ocean in which are afloat every imaginable cuisine — Indian, Mediterranean, Italian, Mexican, Vietnamese, Indonesian, Japanese, Korean, Malaysian, Chinese, Western Grill and many more. It is said that the proof of the pudding is in the eating. If you believe in this adage, give Jiggs Kalra Catering a try.

■ 253, West End Marg, Saidulajaib, Near Garden of 5 Senses, New Delhi, Ph: 9311520712, 9911203077

Jyoti Aggarwal

CONFECTIONERY 9am to 8pm
Food-2.75 | Meal per plate-₹225

Jyoti Aggarwal is an option for those who want to have their cake and eat it too! Her cakes, brownies and fresh fruit tarts are all made with whole wheat and low-fat options. Though she has an interesting choice for those with health problems, she makes no claims about being diabetic-friendly. With a short notice, she can bake you a rather good Chocolate Cake with half the calories that you would normally consume. She also does eggless cakes. For the health conscious, she's the one to turn to. Just remember to order 24 hours in advance with a minimum order of a 1kg cake. She also takes cooking classes and conducts food walks in the city.

■ C 511, Sheikh Sarai I, New Delhi, Ph: 26011136, 9811132450

Kamla Lal

MULTI-CUISINE (Indian, Chinese, Burmese, Lebanese, Thai, Mexican, European) 24Hours
Food- 3.00 | Meal per plate-₹325

Kamla provides full meals, all the way from breakfast to dinner. This caterer also specializes in birthday parties, for which she bakes a variety of cakes and makes mini sandwiches, burgers, pizzas and quiches. Her Mezze is worth a shot, too. Kamla's Burmese fare is also worth a try. Recommended for special parties at home when the gathering is between two and twenty persons. Just remember to order 24 hours in advance. The food has to be picked up from her address in your own containers.

■ S 69, Panchsheel Park, New Delhi, Ph: 26017705, 26016517, 41024451, 9810299865

Kashmiri Food Centre

INDIAN (Kashmiri) 24Hours
Food-3.50 | Meal per plate-₹300

You don't have to be in the verdant Valley to have your fill of Rogan Josh, Yakhni, Methi Chaman and Kabargah. You can have all this at Anita Agha's Kashmiri Food Centre. The menu is fairly representative of Kashmiri cuisine and includes vegetarian and non-vegetarian that the Pandits are famous for. Try the Yakhni, the sausage-shaped Mutton Koftas and the Kabargah. The Gular Kebabs with their stuffing of mint chutney and raisins are excellent. For the vegetarian, the Khatti Arhar Dal, Zimikand Kebab and Tomato Chaman are a must-have. Order four days in advance over the telephone and pick up your stuff as there is no delivery service.

■ 9811209097

Kayalan

MALAY
11am to 11pm
Food-2.75 | Meal per plate-₹400

The neat, not-too-large menu offered by Kayalan gives you a fair representation of the original! The absence, at any rate, of the predictable can be found in the Otak Otak, the most delicate steamed fish, with a whiff of coconut, encased in banana leaf with a distinct flavour and aroma. Excellent — go for it. The more ubiquitous Pandan Chicken is just about passable. The Satay, which is not quite the Indonesian-Thai original, is worth trying. A must-order is the Curry Laksa — the closest that can taste to the Peranakan or Nonya original. Worth a try is the Char Kway Teow, flat noodles done in Chinese-inspired style which end up more like a chicken-prawn Phad noodle dish. They serve food that stays with you the morning after, but it's honest; it's reasonable; it's a great change. Kayalan provides home delivery.

B 113, Freedom Fighter Enclave, Ignou Road, New Delhi, Ph: 9310219192

Kiran Bhushi

SOUTH INDIAN, GOAN
Food-3.25

A sociologist with an abiding interest in food, Kiran is clear about one thing: she does not have a menu, nor will she prepare one. As she hails from Andhra Pradesh, South Indian food is part of her oeuvre, but rather than being straitjacketed by geographical boundaries, she takes inspiration from a variety of sources. You can have a home-made thick dosa made by her that has resonances with a Goan *ale-bele*, and that is the essence of her cooking. It is also the reason why she doesn't have a menu: she wants to be able to tune in on the mood of her customer and plan something exciting and custom-made on the spur of the moment. Her minimum order is for — hold your breath — one person, and the maximum is for 20. She will come to your house and cook a meal for a few guests, or cook the food in her house and have it picked up by you.

Asian Games Village, Ph: 9899125587

Kitchen Art Company, The

MULTI-CUISINE (Indian, Andhra, Chinese, Greek)
Food-3.75

Ask 20 of the city's movers and shakers about their last party: chances are that the name Puneet Sikand will crop up frequently. Sikand has worked in two of Delhi's top hotels and has a finely honed sense of what top-flight parties ought to have on their menus. He prides himself on not having a single speciality, but can do Andhra dishes, Greek food and Chinese with equal facility. Much copied, his menu is listed on his website and must rank as the most plagiarized menu in the city today. You can, of course, download the name 'supplie' but how many people know that this little fried morsel is made with Arborio rice with a nugget of mozzarella in it? And that when the guest bites into it, the cheese stretches into a wire, called 'supplie' in Italian? But ask Sikand to give you a formal corporate party and a wedding in Ludhiana, and both sets of guests will have the time of their lives. Website: www.tkac.in.

Khasra 447, Jonapur, Mehrauli, New Delhi, Ph: 26658533/36, 9810011678

Mala Bindra

CONFECTIONERY 9am to 7.30pm
Food-3.25 | ₹700/kg

There are several women in Delhi who do brisk business in cakes and desserts from their homes. Mala Bindra, one of this tribe, supplies only cakes in five flavours — Chocolate, Orange, Mocha, Caramel and Pineapple. She has recently added some superb cheesecake, Chocolate Mousse and Coffee Cake to her repertoire. As for the quality, there is only one word to describe the cakes — stunning! Mala's catering service is ideal for small parties when you have too much on your mind but would still like to serve home-made dessert. Do remember Mala requires a two-day notice and a minimum order of a 1kg cake.

■ 2, Palam Marg, 2nd Floor, Vasant Vihar, New Delhi, Ph: 9811039894

Maya Handmade Chocolates

CONFECTIONERY 24Hours
Food-3.50 | Meal per plate-₹225

Abha Kohli makes flavoured chocolates, cakes, and cookies. Most of her cakes are tea cakes like Date & Walnut Cake, Raisin Cake, and Spice Cake made with sweet spices. In addition, she makes Fudgy Brownies, chewy and sticky, Lemon Cake, Plain Chocolate Cake without icing or with frosting in which case it becomes her famous Chocolate Truffle Cake. There is an eggless version of the chocolate cake in both its avatars as well as the Spice Cake. There are chocolates with a home-made coffee liqueur flavour in the soft centre, Rum Raisin, Green Peppercorn Vodka, Salted Butter Caramel Chocolates and many others, depending on your order. Her Shortbread Cookies are made without eggs though only the flavour varies. This too is customized according to your preference, and can include Cinnamon, Chocolate Chip and Lemon. Just before Christmas every year is when she makes a rich plum cake with real Jamaica rum.

■ 1325, Sector D, Pocket I, Vasant Kunj, New Delhi, Ph: 26124191, 9818250010

Nandini and Tarani Khanna

CONFECTIONERY, MULTI-CUISINE (Indian, Italian, European) 24Hours
Food-3.00 | Meal per plate-₹400

Nandini and Tarani Khanna are twin sisters who have different areas of operation. One does main courses: Western and North Indian and the other does desserts. They do an interesting Opera Cake, Tiramisu and Cheese Cake. But for bake's sake, they offer a lot more than just desserts. They go the whole hog: Tarani's Roast Chicken and Rack of Lamb are pretty good. The Kasoori Methi Chicken and Kozhi Varutha Curry are not bad; the Pastas and Lasagne competent. The Mezze and Kebabs make for interesting variety as well. The duo is good at their work and won't disappoint you, but a 24-hour notice is a must.

■ D 199, Defence Colony, New Delhi, Ph: 24694070, 41555744, 9811099288, 9711331164

Neelam Sihouta

INDIAN (Kashmiri) 10am to 6pm
Food-3.00 | Meal per plate-₹600

Neelam Sihouta offers her catering services on request and can handle large parties, if given a minimum two-day notice. Neelam specializes in Kashmiri fare such as Gushtaba, Rista, Marchwangon Korma, Chicken Yakhni, Kofta, Dum Aloo, Haaq and Dhania Paneer. A good option for those who want to savour the taste of the verdant Valley without going to Kashmir or, for that matter, even stepping out of home! Just remember to order 48 hours in advance, with a minimum order for 15 persons.

■ **D 417, Defence Colony, New Delhi, Ph: 24601447, 9810209826**

Neeru Sahni

CONFECTIONERY 8am to 8pm
Food-3.25 | ₹500/kg

The secret recipe of Neeru Sahni's successful tryst with taste is the passion with which she bakes her cakes. The secret of her success is the few cakes that she offers: she has gained mastery over them in the long years she has been making them. Her Chocolate Cake, Coffee Cake and Chocolate Praline Cake are all recommended, but her Chocolate Praline Cake, served as it is in a ring mould, is special only to her. You can also try the Chocolate Praline Cake in the eggless variety. Certainly recommended. Do remember, a minimum order of a 1kg cake, and 24 hours' notice is required.

■ **8, Sri Ram Road, Civil Lines, New Delhi, Ph: 23985563, 9811511115**

Niloufer Dhondy

MULTI-CUISINE (Indian-Parsi, European), **CONFECTIONERY** 9am to 6.30pm
Food-3.00 | Meal per plate-₹750

Niloufer Dhondy is somewhat of a jack-of-all-trades and a master of some. Baking is what she is best at. She does regular cakes as well — try her Rich Chocolate Cake, with generous garnishes of cocoa and marzipan, Carrot Cake and Pineapple Upside Down Cake. Also recommended is her Parsi fare, especially her Dhansak, Sali Boti, Patrani-Machchh and Prawn Patia. She requires a minimum order of 1kg cake and two days' advance notice.

■ **C 2/57, Sushant Lok I, Gurgaon, Ph: 9810173833**

Prabha Gulati

MULTI-CUISINE (Indian, Chinese, Burmese, European)
CONFECTIONERY 9am to 9pm
Food-3.00 | Meal per plate-₹400

Prabha Gulati is as much in demand for her Apple Pies and Guava Cheesecakes as she is for her Bhuna Meat and her Khao Suey. One of the better caterers in East Delhi, Prabha includes Thai Curries, pastas and Lasagne in her repertoire as well. However, there is a catch: Prabha does not cater for more than 60 persons or less than 20 and needs a minimum three days' notice.

■ **SDF 38 A, Sector 15A, Noida, Ph: 0120-4334253, 2511852**

Preah Narang

EUROPEAN, ICE-CREAM, SNACKS, CONFECTIONERY — 9am to 7pm
Food-4.00 | Meal per plate-₹400

Preah is a passionate cook and extends her catering expertise to high-profile parties. French food, fresh fruit sorbets, quiches and desserts are Preah's speciality. While she has that special touch which makes for the most important ingredient in any preparation, Preah's Chocolate and Coffee Ice-creams are worth trying.

■ 23, Prithviraj Road, Flat 3B, Tata Apartments, New Delhi, Ph: 24617115, 24617026, 9810007997

Prima Kurien

10am to 8.30pm
KERALITE
Food- 3.75

Prima Kurien has her finger in many pies, of which cooking the food of her community — the Syrian Christians of Kerala is only one. She accepts home catering, for which she can email you her menu. Consisting of Meat/Prawn Ularthiyathu, a spectacularly simple yet delicious Avial and a few of the fish curries of Central Kerala, her food is that happy medium between home cooking at its best and restaurant food: the finish is too perfect to be cooked at home! At extra cost, she will have the food delivered to your house and have her assistant make *appams* in your kitchen, the better to demolish some seriously good Meen Moilee. She prides herself on her Pork Vindaloo, yet her vegetarian dishes are as delicious as anything that comes out of her kitchen. Minimum order that Prima takes is for ₹1,000. You need to give her a notice of 24 hours or even more depending on the size of the order. Pay a delivery charge ranging between ₹150 and ₹600, depending on where you are located. You can also reach Prima through email: *primakurien42@yahoo.com.*

■ Ph: 9811820074

Radhika Sehgal

CONFECTIONERY — 9am to 8pm
Food-3.00 | ₹350/kg

Radhika Sehgal boasts of a degree in catering from Culinary Institute of America, San Francisco, which makes her a professionally qualified patissiere. She bakes the cakes herself and offers a variety of deceptively simple Pineapple, Carrot, Strawberry, Banana, Coconut and Fruit Cakes. But it's the Chocolate Mousse Cake that is the real winner here. If you give Radhika a 24-hour notice, you can be sure to get a luscious, beautifully decorated cake. Go ahead, plan your life — it's worth it! Radhika doesn't disappoint anytime.

■ B 29, Kailash Colony, New Delhi, Ph: 9811103280

Renu Malhotra

CONFECTIONERY — 10am to 7pm
Food-3.25 | Meal per plate-₹300

Renu Malhotra knows what gets the pulse of birthday boy or girl racing. Her speciality is baking birthday cakes in all shapes and sizes for children. Whether it is a Barbie cake for a little girl or a shape cake of the moment for a boy, Renu has a cake for every child. After half a lifetime of catering to children's parties, Renu knows what works best and has regular supplies of edible colour for icing and sprinkles and sparkles to delight a small child. But Renu's repertoire extends beyond just cakes in unusual shapes. She does cookies, brownies, sandwiches and other no-fuss, simple, appealing and tasty options for children's birthday parties. An option for parents trying to give their child an unforgettable birthday!

Renu's Magic Oven, R 79, Greater Kailash I, New Delhi, Ph: 26418337, 9811500991

Rina Dhawan

CONFECTIONERY 24Hours
Food-3.00 | Meal per plate-₹300

Rina Dhawan has made quite a name for herself in the catering business. Her home-made cakes are served at conferences and fashion shows; and many restaurants have outsourced their desserts to her. Rina's Quiches, Asparagus Rolls, Chocolate Desserts, Cheese and Walnut Cakes are good, but it's their presentation that wins hands-down. She uses a special deco paste to make her preparations look as good as they taste. Worth trying out. Do remember to order a day in advance, with a minimum order of a 1kg cake.

E 43, Greater Kailash Enclave, 2nd Floor, New Delhi, Ph: 26242517, 9868025049

Shabeena's Home to Home

INDIAN (Awadhi) 9am to 9pm
Food-3.50 | Meal per plate-₹200

There are a few places in the city which serve authentic home-style Muslim food, the kind which is served at some of the finest homes during Eid or at a traditional Muslim wedding. But Shabeena Naseem, whose takeaway-cum-home delivery outfit has rechristened itself as Homes to Homes, provides the flavours and aromas of those wonderful Biryanis, Kormas and kebabs. The very affordable Shami Kebabs here, the Lucknowi Mutton Biryani and the Koftas are highly recommended for those special parties when you are expecting a number of people. However, Shabeena Naseem needs your order a day in advance.

103/11, Shahjahanabad, Plot 1, Sector 11, Phase I, Dwarka, New Delhi, Ph: 32901206, 9868206932

Sudha Goculdas

10am to 8.30pm
GUJARATI
Food-3.25

Want healthy snacks, Dhoklas and Khandvi that have a certain purity and home-made old-fashioned appeal about them? Look no further than Sudha Goculdas, the matriarch of all things Gujarati. Sticking to completely vegetarian, without onion or garlic, this mistress of spices makes several types of Dhoklas, Khandvi, Theplas, Methi Mattri, Ajwain Matti, Kachoris, Farsaan, Bhelpuri and Shrikhand. Each has the goodness of purity in every bite because Sudha*ji* does this as a labour of love. As good as any professional Farsaan seller on the streets of Ahmedabad, but without the short-cuts, her large client list has been known to pack Farsaan and Theplas on long summer holidays overseas to retain a taste of home! About the only non-Gujarati snack that this remarkable lady does is Cocktail Idlis.

G 262, Palam Vihar, Gurgaon, Ph: 0124-2460421, 9810356891

Sweet Temptations

CONFECTIONERY 9.30am to 9pm

Food-2.75 | Meal per plate-₹200

Preeti Suri's Sweet Temptations tempt you sweetly with Tiramisu, Cheesecakes, Apple Cinnamon Cakes, Chocolate Walnut Brownies, Almond Rock Chocolate.... This made-to-order service does special eggless cakes on request as well. Not a bad option if you want to order dessert for that special dinner at home or when you just don't have the time or inclination. Of late, Sweet Temptations has added savouries such as patties and kebabs to its repertoire as well. Do remember, 24 hours' notice is required.

■ 138, Taimur Nagar, Opp. Gate 4, New Friends Colony, New Delhi, Ph: 64672125, 9810678184

■ 5, D Block Market, Vasant Vihar, New Delhi, Ph: 46012200, 46012402

Temptations

CONFECTIONERY 6am to 9pm

Food-3.25 | ₹500/kg

Specializing in birthday cakes of every design and dimension, Shashi Gupta's cakes are, literally, temptations! Her Chocolate Truffle Cake and Cheesecake are extraordinarily good, with the ingredients used being absolutely fresh. For Mrs Gupta to bake a cake for you, the minimum weight required is 1.5kg. While her cakes and desserts — which can be ordered for parties for 40 to 50 persons — have to be picked up, Mrs Gupta undertakes home delivery at a nominal charge on special request. Mrs Gupta also does elaborate desserts such as Strawberry Paradise — a layer of cake surrounded by chocolate éclairs and filled with Strawberry — and Chocolate Mousse. The embellishments on her cakes and desserts are tasteful and executed with finesse — so, you can admire your cake... and eat it too! Do remember, a minimum order of 1 kg, and 24 hours' notice is required.

■ A 41, Friends Colony East, New Delhi, Ph: 26311917, 26847656

V Cater

INDIAN, INDO-PAK, ITALIAN, CHINESE 10am to 6pm

Food-2.50 | Meal per plate-₹700 Onwards

V Cater has developed a kind of niche marketing, catering to parties thrown by the bigwigs, mostly from the corporate world. Claiming to employ some of the best chefs from around the world — Chinese, Italian, etc. — they say their food is a cut above what the best of caterers have to offer. Although they have ten years' catering experience, they set up shop less than a year ago. V Cater specializes in Indian, Indo-Pak, Italian and Chinese cuisines. Clients are expected to give a notice seven to 50 days ahead of an event and make a down payment of 50 per cent of the total cost.

■ Vatika Triangle, 7th Floor, Sushant Lok 1, Block A, Mehrauli-Gurgaon Road, Gurgaon, Ph: 9560222666

Wicked Temptations

CONFECTIONERY 8am to 7pm
Food-2.75 | Meal per plate-₹350

Wicked Temptations? A delicious name. And Natasha Kapur, the woman behind this made-to-order affair, does a fairly competent job of the cakes and chocolates she hand-makes for her customers. You could also try some of the other wicked temptations that she has on offer — pastries, fruit tarts, Vol-au-Vents.... Wicked? Tempted? Just remember to order 24 hours in advance, with a minimum order of 1kg.

■ UG 9-10, Bhikaji Cama Place, Som Dutt Chambers II, New Delhi, Ph: 26188942

Yummies

CONFECTIONERY 9am to 9pm
Food- 2.75 | Cost: ₹400/Kg

Latika and Geetika Sakhuja are an awesome twosome. Doing what they enjoy most, they have made a profession out of a hobby — just desserts. All they need is a 24-hour notice and a minimum order of a 1kg Cake, and they can whip character-shaped Butter Cookies for you. Her Lemon Cheesecake is pretty good, as are her New York Style Cheese Cake, Coffee Cake and Chocolate Praline Cake. True to its name, Yummies is a yummy option for hassled parents trying to give their child a memorable birthday!

■ E 5, Maharani Bagh, New Delhi, Ph: 41628310, 41628207, 9810790900

PROFESSIONAL HOME CATERERS

A One Caterers

MULTI-CUISINE (Chinese, European, Indian)
Food- 2.50 | Meal per plate-₹200

This caterer's name matches the quality of their catering service. For 12 years A One has been catering to people in the Nauroji Nagar area for birthday parties, anniversaries, family get-togethers, weddings. A veggie meal costs ₹200 and a non-vegetarian meal is priced at ₹300. Chinese, European and Indian cuisines are what you will get at A One Caterers. There is no limit to the number of guests that they can handle with ease. Do not approach them if you have less than 100 guests. A pre-payment of 25 per cent of the total amount is a must. They also need a notice of three days.

A1, Nauroji Nagar, New Delhi, Ph: 26182406, 65163067

Ada-e-Handi

MULTI-CUISINE (European, Chinese, Indian) 11am to 11pm
Food- 2.50

Pankaj Arora has been running catering services for people around Rajinder Nagar for 10 years. Be it a birthday party or a get-together for upto 100 persons or a wedding or an anniversary, he supplies from his kitchen almost all kinds of fare — right from Chhole Bhature to European to Indian to Mughlai cuisine. Up his sleeve are many specials: Afghani Chicken, Murgh Malai, Handi Special, Murgh Reshmi and Shahi Paneer. Ada-e-Handi is capable of serving food for up to a 100 persons. But you need to pay part of the bill in advance.

37/1, Old Rajinder Nagar, Ph: 25851768, 25784504

Adhana Tent House & Caterers

MULTI-CUISINE (Chinese, North Indian, Kashmiri, South Indian) 8am to 8pm
Food- 2.50 | Meal per plate-₹550 onwards

Vijay Adhana caters to more than 100 guests at a time. From a family get-together to an anniversary celebration to a birthday party to a corporate event, this caterer will live up to your expectation. Chinese, European, Thai, North Indian, Kashmiri and South Indian cuisine are what they prepare. The specialities that you get here are Punjabi, Kahmiri and South Indian. One veg plate costs ₹550 while a non-vegetarian meal is priced at ₹650. A down-payment of 50 per cent is required to make a booking, which should be done one month in advance.

Near Kribhco Township, Morna Market, Sector 35, Noida, Ph: 9811722143, 9811946414

All Heavens

MULTI-CUISINE (Chinese, Indian) 9am to 11pm
Food- 2.75

Since 1992 Pradeep Gupta has been running the catering service. He specializes in Indian and Chinese cuisine. All Heavens can cater to as many as 10000 persons but the minimum number of guests at any party should not be less than 500. Part of the payment is to be made in advance. You can also pay through credit cards. You also need to inform them at least a week to a fortnight before the party.

B 97, Wazirpur, Opp. Shalimar Bagh, Ring Road, Delhi, Ph: 27377101, 27377103, 27377104, 27377106

Allied Catering Services

MULTI-CUISINE (Chinese, European, Indian, Mughlai, Thai) 9am to 11pm
Food- 2.50 | Meal per plate-₹700

Allied caters to birthday parties, weddings, anniversaries, family get-togethers and parties hosted by corporate houses. Here you have the option for a customized menu and you can choose from Chinese, European, Indian, Mughlai and Thai cuisines. A vegetarian platter is priced at ₹700 and a non-vegetarian platter costs ₹900. Make a payment of 30 per cent of the total money. You need to provide a notice of two days to one week in advance to ensure that everything falls in place. Allied can cater to parties with guests ranging from 50 to 5000. They have been in the business for five years.

A 128/1, 2nd Floor, Mohammadpur, Bhikaji Cama Place, New Delhi, Ph: 26103797, 9871719774

Amarta Caterers & Tent Decorators

MULTI-CUISINE (Chinese, European, North Indian)
Food- 2.50

Amarta Caterers is no big fish in the catering business in Noida. For a little more than four years they have been catering to parties where the number of guests ranges between 200 and 400. They make delicacies from Chinese, European, North Indian cuisines and work on tailor-made menus. You have to deposit 25 per cent of the total amount in advance. Whether it is a birthday party or an anniversary celebration, Amarta requires a notice of two to three days.

SR Complex, Naya Bans, Sector 15, Noida, Ph: 0120-2511423, 9811162272

Amritsari

NORTH INDIAN 9.30am to 3.30pm, 7pm to 11pm
Food- 2.75

If you want to throw a veg-only party you can call Paramjeet Singh. For almost seven years he has been running catering service at Model Town I area. Be it a wedding or a birthday party or an anniversary, Amritsari can supply food for up to 1,000 persons. Amritsari Naan Kulcha, Sarson ka Saag, Butter Curry Chaamp, Chur-Chur Naan, Dal Makhni and Shahi Paneer are some of the dishes they claim to do well. You have to pay 50 per cent of the cost in cash in advance because they don't accept credit cards.

G 28, DDA Market, Gujranwala Town, Part 1, Delhi, Ph: 65293034

Apni Rasoi

INDIAN (VEG) 11am to 4.30pm, 7pm to 11pm
Food- 2.75

Praveen Kumar Goel, the owner of Apni Rasoi, caters to parties at Rashtrapati Bhavan, for the Delhi Police and some government bodies on a regular basis. But anyone can approach them provided the number of guests ranges between 50 and 100. Let them know about your party in advance and paying 50 per cent of the total amount is a must. It's been eight years of Apni Rasoi.

■ **2489/190, Tota Ram Bazaar, Trinagar, Delhi, Ph: 9212432802**

Aristocrat Caterers & Tent Decorators

Multi-Cuisine (Mughlai, North Indian) 8am to 10pm
Food- 2.50

Apart from providing outdoor tents, Aristocrat Caterers are capable of catering to 200 to 10000 guests. They have a large variety of dishes on offer. And of course you can even go in for a customized menu. They specialize in North Indian and Mughlai cuisine. Soyabean Chaamp, Shukhto, Matar Mushroom, Paneer Razalla, Mutton Kaleji, Musalmani Mutton and Prawn Malai Curry are some of the dishes they are known for. You don't have to deposit money in advance if it is a small order and they promise to deliver at two hours' notice.

■ **Shop No. 9, Market No. 1, Chittaranjan Park, New Delhi, Ph: 9811911325, 9811126246, 9999777901**

■ **35/946, DDA Flats, Kalkaji, New Delhi, Ph: 9811651278**

Ashok Joseph

Multi-Cuisine (Chinese, Mediterranean, European, Italian) 9am to 10pm
Food- 2.75 | **Meal per plate-₹600**

Ashok Joseph is as much in demand for his Seafood Paella and Lamb Chop with Whisky Sauce as he is for his Pan-Roasted Chicken and Prawn Cocktail. The Loin Pork with Brandy and Prune Sauce and Carpaccio are worth a shot too. A popular caterer for many an occasion, you could turn to Ashok Joseph if you plan a biggish party. Just remember to order one week in advance, with a minimum order of 10. And this service is restricted to people living in South Delhi.

■ **Ph: 9818824998**

Ayush Caterers & Decorators

Multi-Cuisine (Indian, North Indian and Mughlai)
Food- 2.50 | **Meal per plate-₹250**

For the last eight years Ayush Caterers & Decorators have been catering to the people of Mayur Vihar Phase III, hosting large get-togethers, birthday bashes and marriage parties. Ayush caters to a minimum of 100 guests but they say they can cater to any number of people. Indian, North Indian and Mughlai cuisines are what they specialize in. Chicken Korma, Mutton Korma, Chicken Biryani, Mutton Rogan Josh and Seekh Kebab are some of the dishes they are known for. A vegetarian meal costs ₹250 and a non-vegetarian one ₹350. You need to pay 20 per cent of the cost in advance.

■ **57A, Pocket A-3, Mayur Vihar, Phase III, Delhi, Ph: 9650872811**

Baboo Shahi Bawarchi

North Indian 9am to 8pm
Food- 2.75 | **Meal per plate-₹300**

At a stone's throw from Pragati Maidan, Baboo Shahi Bawarchi at Matka Pir is an eatery which is also into catering.

They can serve up to 100 to 150 persons at a time. Their menu may not too elaborate but the food is pleasing to the taste buds. They prepare mainly Biryani, Chicken/Mutton Korma, Shami Kebab, Lucknow Aloo Galouti Kebab and Kofta Curry. You don't have to pay anything in advance but notify them at least one to two days before the event. Baboo Shahi Bawarchi has been in business for the last 25 years.

4-5, Dargah Matka Pir, Near Pragati Maidan, New Delhi, Ph: 23371454

Balki Foods

Multi-Cuisine (Chinese, Indian, South Indian) 24 Hrs
Food- 2.50 | Meal for per plate-₹200 onwards

Balki Foods owner Anil Shukla claims to have done catering for some of the top corporate houses. They also cater to birthday parties, weddings, family get-togethers, Diwali dinners and other occasions. Chinese, Indian and South Indian are among the vast array of cuisines they can prepare. A vegetarian meal costs ₹200 and a non-vegetarian one ₹250 and upwards. Whether they have to cater to 25 guests or 12000, they are meticulous about every detail, and neither their food nor service will disappoint you. You need to inform them just two days in advance if the number of guests is not large. Otherwise you should give them a notice of one week to 10 days. They have been catering for the last 25 years.

G 164, Sector 63, Noida, Ph: 9818814131

Bhatia Caterers

Veg
Food- 2.50 | Meal per plate-₹150

Bhatia has been in the catering business for 60 years and they supply vegetarian dishes only. Located as they are in the proximity of the North Campus of Delhi University, it is usually the university seminars they cater at. But they also take orders for weddings and other social events. The cost per plate is ₹160. The Bhatias are capable of handling between 50 and 1000 guests at two to three days' notice.

89 A, Near Bhatia Chowk, Kamla Nagar, Delhi, Ph: 9810185332, 23844845, 23845745, 23845845

Burmese Kitchen

Multi-Cuisine (Burmese, Chinese, Hyderabadi, Morrocan)
Food- 2.75 | Meal per plate-₹300 onwards

Burmese Kitchen mostly serves people in the NCR region of Faridabad and Gurgaon. They generally cater to corporate houses but they are capable of handling any number of guests, whether at homes or offices. You can ask them for Burmese, Chinese, Hyderabadi, Morrocan, South Indian or Thai cuisine. Burmese Kitchen specializes in Lethok, Green Bean, Sesame Salad and Red Gold Pork, all of which are authentic Burmese fare. A vegetarian meal will cost ₹300 and a non-vegetarian meal ₹400. Depending upon the order and the occasion, you need to both notify and pay in advance. For inquiries phone them or visit their website *http://burmesekitchen.in.*

H 16/6, DLF Phase I, Gurgaon, Ph: 0124-4045377

Celebration Caterer & Decorators

MULTI-CUISINE (Chinese, Mexican, Mughlai, North Indian, Thai)
Food- 2.50 | Meal per plate-₹550

Celebration Caterer & Decorators owner Pramod Singh is a seasoned person who has been catering for the last 18 years. There is a considerable repertoire of cuisine that he makes for birthdays, anniversaries, weddings and functions at offices. He prepares Chinese, Mexican, Mughlai, North Indian and Thai cuisines. A vegetarian meal is priced at ₹ 525 per plate and a non-vegetarian meal costs ₹750. You need to deposit 25 per cent of the total money in advance. A notice of two days to one month is required if you have to book for as many 20000 guests and below.

Shop No. 22, D Block Market, Near Sai Baba Mandir, Sector 40, Noida, Ph: 9873584647, 66355384

Chakh Le India

VEG
Food- 2.50 | Meal per plate-₹200

This is a veg-only catering service, operating from the NCR region in Gurgaon for the last three years. Pyaaz Kachori, Dhokla and Srikhand are some of their prized specialities which they serve at parties and lunches for corporates. You have to give them four days' notice and pay 50 per cent in advance. The cost of a meal at Chakh Le is ₹200 and they can cater to 50 to 2000 persons.

Lakshya Building, Ground Floor, Inside MDI, Gurgaon, Ph: 9650631134

Chawla Chicken

MULTI-CUISINE (Indian, Mediterranean)
Food- 2.75

The Chawlas are capable of catering to as few as 50 persons, though there is no limit to the higher number. You need to give two days' notice and make a 50 per cent advance payment. Mutton Chicken, biryani, Shawarma and Chicken Tikka are some of the delicacies that they serve. In the catering business for the last 10 years, they claim the American Embassy to be one of their special clients.

S No. 1, Central Market, Behind Green Field School, Safdarjung Enclave, New Delhi, Ph: 9899114173

Chef Khan — The Kitchen

MULTI-CUISINE (Indian, Italian, Mexican, Lebanese, Swiss, European, Thai, Indonesian) 9am to 10pm
Food-2.75 | Meal per plate-₹200

Khan's European fare is rather good, especially the salads, Cheese Steak and pasta counter. You could try the Yakitori, Soga Noodles, Red, Green and Yellow Curry, and Prawn Curry that Chef Khan does competently. The Indian, unfortunately, doesn't transcend beyond Paneer Lababdar, Malai Gobhi, Mutton Seekh Kebab, Kadhai Chicken, Dal 'Bukhara' and Chicken Biryani. Catering to both convenience and culinary tastes, Chef Khan is a possible choice on evenings when you want to entertain outdoors, but don't want to cook indoors! A minimum order for 25 persons, and two days' advance notice is what he requires.

■ 29, DDA Market, Ashram, New Delhi, Ph: 65974141, 9810350466, 9810350847

Chefs United

MULTI-CUISINE (Indian, European, Italian, Mexican, Thai, Greek, Moroccan, Arabian, Lebanese) 9am to 6pm

Food- 3.00 | Meal per plate-₹400

Sunil Chauhan is an efficient caterer. Sunil's catering company, Chefs United, provides the cutlery, the waiters and all the other frills for the party you want to have but are too intimidated to organize. Fab India, Oxford and Cambridge Society of India, the British Council Division, Australian High Commission, German School, German Embassy and Aus Aid are his clients. Chauhan himself is a chef, one of the few people in the catering business to be so qualified. You could try the Teriyaki Fish, Galouti Kebab, Grill Lobsters, Paneer Dhaniya Adraki, Paneer Kofta, Steamed Fish in Banana Leaf and Red Chicken Curry. Among the desserts, dig into Malai Ke Paan, Jauzi Halwa, Chocolate Nougat Cake, Sheer Brinj and Baileys Irish Cheese Cake. Do remember, a minimum order of 50 and one month's notice is required.

■ 2028/19, Pilanji, Main Road, Kotla Mubarakpur, New Delhi, Ph: 24654005, 9810148936, 981050477, 9650897440

Chinese Hot Momos & Caterers

CHINESE

Food- 2.50 | Meal per plate-₹200

This is a small-time caterer in that they do small orders — not more than 20 to 30 guests. They make Chinese cuisine and momos exclusively and seem to be good at doing that. A meal that you shall order with Chinese Hot will cost you ₹200. You can ask for all varieties of momos — veggie, chicken and mutton. They also make dim sums. You need to inform them one or two days prior to your party so that they are able to deliver on time. Chinese Hot Momos have been catering for the last three years.

■ D 137/8, Near Gulmohar Park Road, Gautam Nagar, New Delhi, Ph: 9810462925

Cost Effective Catering

MULTI-CUISINE

Food- 2.50 | Meal per plate-₹200 onwards

Ankit, the proprietor of this catering service, claims that whatever they serve is not only special but also cost-effective. They have been catering at parties, weddings and other events. They serve mostly multi-cuisine food. A vegetarian meal costs ₹200 and a non-vegetarian ₹400. There is no upper limit of guests they can cater to but the lower limit is set at 100. And you will do well to give them two weeks' notice. Cost Effective Catering has been in business for 10 years now.

■ 32 UB, Jawahar Nagar, Kamla Nagar, Delhi, Ph: 9312218363, 9210442464

Dawat Caterers

MULTI-CUISINE (Chinese, Indian, European, Arabian) 9am to 6pm
Food- 2.50 | Meal per plate-₹400 onwards

For 22 years Sameer Saxena has been catering for birthday parties, anniversaries, family get-togethers, Diwali dinners, and corporate parties in South Delhi localities. Arabian, Chinese, Indian, European and Mexican cuisines are what they claim to excel in. Whether you have 50 or 1500 guests at your party, Sameer takes care of the minutest details. You need to make a down-payment of 50 per cent at the time of booking. A notice of 24 hours will do if you are throwing a small party. But if you have more guests let them know much in advance so that they can make proper arrangments.

■ B 53/1, DDA Flats, East of Kailash, New Delhi, Ph: 9810110780, 26911784

Deep Sons

MULTI-CUISINE (Indian, Chinese) 9am to 9pm
Food- 2.25 | Meal per plate-₹400

This is somewhat of a *sasta* and *kifayati* option for catering in Indian and Chinese fare. With ubiquitous Dal Makhni, Kadhai Chicken, Kadhai Paneer, Mutton Rogan Josh and *chalu* Chinjabi fare — Manchurian, Chilli Paneer, Chilli Chicken — on offer, there's nothing great to expect. Still, the prices are friendly and the serving portions relatively large.

■ 23/2, Chhoti Subzi Mandi, Janakpuri, New Delhi, Ph: 65140207, 9810569616

Dua F & B Outdoors & Events Management

MULTI-CUISINE (Chinese, Japanese, Italian, European) 8am to 8pm
Food-2.50 | Meal per plate-₹200

A popular caterer for many an occasion, Food and Beverage Catering Services is what you could turn to if you plan a biggish party with regular buffet fare. Grilled Fish with Teriyaki Sauce, Grilled Prawns, Chicken Lababdar, Tikkas, kebabs.... With the staple fare of both Indian and European cuisine being available, the menu might not be too experimental, but it is exhaustive — just the buffer for a buffet! Do remember, a minimum order for 100 persons and a two-day notice is required.

■ Kh. No. 627, Chandanhola, Fatehpur Beri, New Delhi, Ph: 26653666, 9810130012, 9810246888, 9810117943

Durbar Restaurant

MULTI-CUISINE (North Indian, Chinese, European) 11am to 11pm
Food- 2.50 | Meal per plate-₹100 onwards

From time to time the threshold to Durbar Restaurant in Mayur Vihar Phase I is beautifully lighted and decorated with festoons. It is a place where people of this locality host parties — kitty parties to birthdays to anniversaries to family get-togethers to any other occasion in the family. Whether you want your party to be hosted at this venue or not Durbar will cater for you. They offer a wide range of chicken and mutton dishes such as Tangdi Kebab, Aachari Tikka, Afghani Chicken and Mutton Roghan Josh. The Paneer Tikka, served as a sizzler, is nice. They also prepare vegetarian dishes. You have to deposit part of the total money in advance and this maount might vary from one client to another. Give a notice of at least two days to one week. They can cater to as many as 150 persons. Credit cards are accepted.

▪ 166 A, Pratap Nagar, Mayur Vihar, Phase I, Delhi, Ph: 22752148, 9818336611

Easy India Services & Mozaic

MULTI-CUISINE (Lebanese, Mediterranean)
Food- 3.25 | Meal per plate-₹400 onwards

Apart from catering to celebrities in the posh Vasant Vihar locality of South Delhi, Easy India Services has the distinction of preparing food for functions held in embassies located in this area. Although Lebanese and Mediterranean cuisines are what they do best, you can try out other delicacies too. They provide customized menu for birthdays, anniversaries, weddings, etc. and can easily cater to 500 guests. One plate costs between ₹400 and ₹ 500. You need to make the booking one week in advance. Deposit 65 per cent of the total money when you book.

▪ E 8/15, Vasant Vihar, New Delhi, Ph: 9990775454, 9818775454

Elegant Caterers

MULTI-CUISINE (Chinese, Indian, Italian, Mexican, Mughlai)
Food- 2.50 | Meal per plate-₹500 onwards

The proprietor of Elegant Caterers, Suneet has been running the catering business for a decade. They can handle any number of guests but the minimum limit is 30. Here you have a wide choice — Chinese, Indian, Italian, Mexican, Mughlai and Thai cuisines. Lasagne, Walnut Brownies, Galouti Kebab and Kakori Kebab are some of their specialties. A notice of two days and an advance payment of up to 80 per cent are needed. A vegetarian meal costs ₹550 and a non-vegetarian nothing less than ₹750.

▪ 405, 2nd Floor, H 17A, Main Road, Kalkaji, New Delhi, Ph: 9811137808, 9873446363

Empire Caterers

MULTI-CUISINE (Chinese, European, Indian, Italian)
Food- 2.50 | Meal per plate-₹400 onwards

With 12 years' experience under its belt, Empire today is an established caterer to corporate offices. Whether it is a small gathering of 50 persons or a big event with a presence of 2000, Empire can handle the catering with equal efficiency. They provide Chinese, European, Indian and Italian fare. Two of their specialities are Biryani and Kathi Roll. A vegetarian meal costs ₹400 and a non-vegetarian ₹650. Two days' notice and an advance payment of 50 per cent are required to service an order.

▪ 55, Palika Bazar, Connaught Place, New Delhi, Ph: 9971791606, 9971792606

Feeding Concepts, The

MULTI-CUISINE (Awadhi, North Indian, South Indian, Chinese, Thai) 24Hrs
Food- 2.50

The Feeding Concepts owner Ujjwal Gogia is a caterer with a difference. From birthday parties for children to cocktail parties to Diwali dinners to stag parties to wedding feasts to poolside parties, they prepare custom-made menus for all occasions. They make a variety of cuisines — Awadhi, North Indian, South Indian, Chinese, Thai, etc. Dishes like Galouti Kebab, Ocean Blue Crabs, Sushi and Cheese Platter are among their specialities. Feeding Concepts caters for not less than 20 guests. But even if there are 1000 persons, they will do a good job. Pay 50 per cent of the total money in advance, and book your order 10 days prior to your event.

City Square Mall, Rajouri Garden, New Delhi, Ph: 9810014550, 9810994332

Grand F&B Catering Services

MULTI-CUISINE (European, French, Japanese, Lebanese, Mexican, Thai) 11am to 10pm
Food- 3.00

Run by NP Nanda, Grand F&B Catering Services claims to be the best catering service in Delhi and the NCR region. They offer their service to corporates, weddings and other outdoor events. F&B serves European, French, Mexican, South Indian and Chinese cuisine. They also have branded counters like special low-calorie food but this comes at a premium. They have a website (*http://www.grandfnb.com*) which will introduce you to the various options available here. You have to make a down-payment of 10 per cent before you place an order, which should be done two days in advance. This caterer can handle between 100 and 3000 persons and won't let you down.

Rajouri Garden, Delhi, Ph: 9811700027, 9811805377

Harisons

MULTI-CUISINE (Indian, Japanese, Thai)
Food- 2.75 | Meal per plate-₹400 onwards

Rohit Rai has been running Harisons for the last 43 years. He has been catering mostly to the corporates and he can handle 100 to 2000 guests. But he also caters to weddings, anniversaries, birthday parties, small or big family get-togethers, Diwali dinners, etc. Of course, you need to tell him in advance but all depends on when you are holding the party. You can pay as much as 20 per cent in advance. Sushi, Thai and Indian are some of the cuisines that Harisons will serve for you. A vegetarian platter costs ₹450 and a non-vegetarian one ₹550.

30G, Marina Arcade, Connaught Place, New Delhi, Ph: 9811035325, 9811035375, 9868105686

Honey Dew

CONFECTIONERY 24Hours
Food- 3.00 | Meal per plate-₹300

This one is a hit with the kids. Vandana Singh knows what gets the pulse of the birthday boy or girl racing. Be it Irish Coffee Mousse, Chocolate Rum Dessert, Molten Lava Cake, Almond Date Blondie or Butter Scotch Blondie, Vandana has them all. Her Love in the Mist, Rockie Road and Nutty Surprise are worth a shot too. With a freshness that is missing in neighbourhood bakeries and up-market patisseries, Honey

Dew is an option for the sweet-toothed. A minimum order of a 1kg cake and 24 hours' notice is what she requires.

504/40, Heritage City, Next to MGF Metropolitan Mall, MG Road, Gurgaon, Ph: 0124-4222290, 9810384284

Hungry NCR.com

MULTI-CUISINE (Chinese, Indian, Mughlai)
Food- 2.50 | Meal per plate-₹ 150 onwards

They have been in catering business in the Gurgaon area for the last three years. Chinese, Indian, Mughlai and multi-cuisine are what they specialize in. Hungry NCR.com is capable of catering to 50 to 1000 persons. Achari Chicken and Achari Veg are some of their specialties. These apart, their dessert is also passable. A veg platter costs ₹150 while a non-veg platter ₹300. You have to pay 30 per cent in advance and give one week's notice. Hungry NCR.com boasts of a number of corporates as their clients.

H No. 4295, Sector 23 A, Gurgaon, Ph: 9811467652, 4060000

Kaushik Sweets & Caterers

MULTI-CUISINE (Chinese, European, Indian, South Indian) 8am to 8pm
Food- 2.50 | Meal per plate-₹ 100 onwards

Kaushik Sweets have been catering for birthdays, weddings, etc. for the last 25 years. Chinese, European, Indian and South Indian cuisines are what they make well. If you engage them for catering you will not have to go to a *mithaiwala* for ordering sweets. Gulab Jamun and Gajar ka Halwa are their most popular ones. They can cater for 100 guests to 5000. One has to book one month in advance and make a down-payment of 50 per cent.

Vanshika Garden, Palam Vihar Raod, Delhi, Ph: 9212055923, 9213764643

Kapoor Tent & Caterers

MULTI-CUISINE (Chinese, Rajasthani, Kashmiri, North Indian) 24Hours
Food- 2.50

Kapoor caters for small parties at home like family get-togethers, birthdays and anniversaries where the number of guests does not exceed 50. Chinese, European, Kashmiri, North Indian, Rajasthani and South Indian cuisines are what Kapoor serves. They can tailor a customized menu to your choice. You have to pay 25 per cent of the total money in advance and you also need to give a week's notice. They have been catering in the Vikas Puri area for the last 25 years.

G 3, Bharti Towers, Vikas Puri, New Delhi, Ph: 28540537, 9312312255

Khushi Caterers

MULTI-CUISINE (Chinese, European, Indian, North Indian, South Indian, Rajasthani, Lebanese, Mexican) 10am to 6pm
Food- 2.75

Gautam Singhnia has been catering for weddings, get-togethers, anniversaries and birthday parties for the last two years. European, South Indian, North Indian, Chinese, Lebanese, Rajasthani, Lucknowi, Mughlai, Thai, Mexican and Mongolian are among the vast array of cuisines that they prepare. They also make cakes, faluda, fruit chaat, health drinks and ice creams. Khushi Caterers can provide food for 100 to 2000 guests. Pay part of the cost in advance when you make the booking, and you need to give at least a week's notice.

■ Near Civil Lines Metro Station, Civil Lines, Delhi, Ph: 9999250353

Kumar Caterers

NORTH INDIAN, SOUTH INDIAN
Food- 2.75 | Meal per plate-₹150 onwards

If you are fond of the cuisine down South, you could turn to Kumar Caterers, which specializes in authentic South Indian food for marriages, parties and religious functions. Kumar has his own way of doing his dishes, which is quite delicious. Idiapam, Appam, Malabar Parootha, Adai, Kadavadi, Pazam Pori, Mysore Masala Dosa.... While the food might not be five-star fare, it's 'zimble' enough for a fulfilling meal. Among others Kumar caters to lunches and dinners hosted at central government offices in New Delhi. For prices ranging between ₹150 and 550 per plate, you can expect a wholesome to a lavish meal. Whether it is 50 persons or 100, Kumar acquit themselves well. With an advance payment of 30 per cent and 10 days' notice you can place your order. Kumars also give you a customized menu with exclusive cuisines from both North and South India. And for a change you may also have some special Indian and Rajasthani food.

■ J3/170, DDA Flats, Kalkaji, New Delhi, Ph: 26027675, 26021657, 9811968681, 9811060440

Lime & Chilli

MULTI-CUISINE (Chinese, Japanese, Rajasthani, Thai)
Food- 2.75 | Meal per plate-₹500 onwards

This catering house has been serving both vegetarian and non-vegetarian fare for private occasions for six years. Chinese, Japanese, Rajasthani and Thai food are what they can serve for as few as 50 persons and as many as 1,500. Kadak Seekh Kebab, Jugalbandi Kebab (Mutton n Chiken Seekh) and Tandoori Shakarkandi are their speciality. A vegetarian platter costs ₹500 and a non-vegetarian ₹800. If you are throwing a party you need to tell them two to three days prior to the event. You can also reach them on limenchilly@gmail.com

■ 47, Community Centre, East Of Kailash, New Delhi, Ph: 9873337779, 9871622279

Maharaja Caterers

MULTI-CUISINE (Chinese, North India, South India)
Food- 2.50 | Meal per plate-₹350 onwards

Jagdish Khemani can cater for 1000 to 5000 persons with different delicacies from Chinese, North India, South India cuisine. The cost for a meal begins at ₹350. You need to tell him at least one week in advance about your menu. He will ask for a deposit of 50 per cent of the total money. Maharaja Caterers has been in the business for 22 years.

■ 7A/9, WEA, Channa Market, Karol Bagh, Near Metro Station, New Delhi, Ph: 25723563, 25723083, 9312231016

Mannat Caterers & Restaurant

MULTI-CUISINE (Chinese, Indian, Italian)
Food- 2.50 | Meal per plate-₹275 onwards

Three years into catering for corporate houses, Anuj Bajaj has been running Mannat Caterers & Restaurant which serves Chinese, Indian and Italian cuisine. They specialize in Dum Biryani, Kathi Roll, Chicken Korma and Kathal Biryani. Mannat are comfortable with parties for persons between 40 and 600. A vegetarian meal per plate will cost ₹275 and a non-vegetarian ₹375. Two days' notice is what they expect to be able to do their job. China Zing restaurant and Toss Bar at Huda Commercial Complex are also owned by the proprietors of Mannat.

■ **SCO No 63, Sector 56, Huda Commercial Complex, Near Appolo Clinic, Gurgaon, Ph: 9818331010, 4116600**

Mozaic Culinary Art Catering & Consultancy

MULTI-CUISINE (Lebanese, Syrian, Mediterranean, Greek) 24Hours
Food-3.50 | Meal per plate-₹500

If you want a bit of Arabia right in your living room, try Raffi, a Syrian national, who offers a made-to-order offering of hot and cold mezze like Hummus, Falafel, Tabbouleh, Baba Ghanoush and Muhammara. Shawarma is the speciality of Raffi and his team of helpers, and during a catered event, it is a common sight to see a line of ambassadors from all over the Middle East patiently standing in line to partake of this melt-in-the-mouth treat at Raffi's stall. All his dishes are worth trying, even the rarely seen fish-based dishes. As he has been in the business for over a decade, he has his finger on the pulse of what his clients want, both Indian and Middle Eastern, and it is the rare Middle Eastern catered party that does not have Raffi's food! Ramzan is his busiest time of the year, with at least one Iftaar party an evening. A call to Rafi for his catering service is a good way of experiencing Arabian food the way it is meant to be enjoyed. Just remember to order 24 hours in advance.

■ **E 8/15, Vasant Vihar, New Delhi, Ph: 9818775454, 9868122963**

■ **C 7, Masoodpur Market, Vasant Kunj, New Delhi, Ph: 26139001, 9717775454, 9818775454**

Mughal Foods

INDIAN (Lucknawi) 10am to 10pm
Food-3.00 | Meal per plate-₹800

Mughal Foods is one of Delhi's best kept secrets. It is the joint enterprise of Shaad Khan and Azhar Wazari, both gourmets and gourmands from Eastern UP who, with the help of a band of khansamas, provide the rare breed of the rich-and-famous-with-taste in Delhi a glimpse of the real thing, at relatively affordable prices. The highlight of Mughal Foods remain the Kakoris and the Galoutis — both are gentle, melt-in-the-mouth interpretation, with subtle aromas and flavours. The Yakhni Pullao is a disappointment though. This is *chalu* stuff that goes by the name of Biryani in every neighbourhood market. In contrast, the Haleem, though floating in about three inches of oil, is certainly not bad. The Nihari is passable but the Shabdeg worth a shot and not to be missed. The Murgh Mussalam is distinctive with its special khus-khus and gari flavours. It is certainly worth trying out. Do try the Sheermal; it would give Karim's a run for its money. The Roomali is also done well by Mughal Foods — thin and cooked perfectly. Mughal Foods to lovers of Awadhi cuisine is highly recommendable. It is, for the most part, an honest rendition — particularly in the kebabs department.

■ **E 26, Khizrabad, Near New Friends Colony, New Delhi,
Ph: 9811077861, 9810026218**

Mukta Khetan

SNACKS
Food- 3.50

A Marwari housewife, Mukta Khetan makes a whole range of products. Some are ready-to-eat snacks of the sort that keep for up to three months. Chidva, which is heavily spiked with dry fruits, Kalmi Vadas, Plain and Methi Matthis and Theplas come under this category. For their mithai and namkeens they use pure ghee and some of their fare such as Matar Kachori can be kept for three days. Finally, their main courses, cooked by a maharaj, taste like home-made food. Ker Sangri, a tangy Gatta Curry, and Aloo Gravy, seasoned with hing, are said to very delicious. All food has to be picked up from her residence in your own containers. A minimum of 24 hours' notice needs to be given. When summer begins, Mukta gets busy, with select customers ordering long-lasting snacks for their European sojourns!

■ **First Floor, H 36, Kailash Colony, New Delhi,
Ph: 9818305293**

Naveen Mittal Caterers

MULTI-CUISINE (Indian, Chinese, European) 10am to 5pm
Food- 2.50 | Meal per plate-₹350

Naveen's Marwari sweets are rather good, especially Badam Dal Halwa, Kesariya Imarti, Malpua Khurchan and Meerut Ka Halwa. You could also try the Dal Pachmela, Gatta Jaipuri, Kerr Sangria and Dal Bati Churma that Naveen does competently. He does Kashmiri and Gujarati dishes on request too. The Chinese, unfortunately, doesn't transcend beyond Chicken Manchurian and Chicken Chopsuey. The European fare he offers is iffy. Catering to both convenience and culinary tastes, Naveen is a possible choice when you are expecting a number of people and are in no mood to cook. A minimum order for 50 persons and 24 hours advance notice is what he requires.

■ **879, Kucha Patiram, Bazaar Sita Ram, New Delhi,
Ph: 32601863, 65351382**

Pakwaan Caterers

INDIAN
Food- 2.50 | Meal per plate-₹ 500 onwards

Pakwaan have been catering for ten years for wedding, birthday and kitty parties and for corporate houses in Karol Bagh and other localities. And they are capable of handling guests numbering between 200 and 1000. All they need to serve you is 24 hours' notice, whatever the occasion. A veg platter comes for ₹500 and a non-vegetarian for ₹750. Grapes

Vegetable, Paneer Makhni, Chicken Tikka and Biryani are some of their dishes you may try.

■ **465, Joshi Road, Near Ajmal Khan Park, Karol Bagh, New Delhi, Ph: 9810598680**

Phulwaris Carering Services

Multi-Cuisine (Chinese, Indian, Mughlai)
Food- 2.50 | Meal per plate-₹ 100 onwards

Amandeep Singh, who runs Phulwaris, can provide food for birthday parties, marriage parties and other events where 50 to 500 guests are invited. Phulwaris need a notice of one to five days. They do Chinese, Indian and Mughlai fare. A vegetarian meal costs ₹100 and a non-vegetarian one ₹250. Phulwaris have been in business for six years.

■ **J 10/38, Rajouri Garden, New Delhi, Ph: 9212013853, 9818103563**

Priya Caterers

Multi-Cuisine (Chinese, Indian, Mughlai)
Food- 2.75 | Meal per plate-₹150 onwards

Meena Takkar's Priya Caterers have been running their service at Nehru Enclave for seven years. Chinese, Indian, Mughlai and multi-cuisine food are all available for people hosting parties at home or organizing lunches in offices. It is mostly corporate offices which she caters to mostly, though. Masala Channa, Kashmiri Aloo, Chicken Biryani and Butter Chicken are their best fare. A veggie platter costs ₹150 and a non-vegetarian one ₹200. This caterer can handle as few as 25 persons and as many as 300. A notice of one week is needed to service an order.

■ **1/10, Nerhu Place, Nehru Enclave, New Delhi, Ph: 26434713**

Red Coral Restaurant & Home Caterers

Multi-Cuisine (Rajasthani, Mexican, Punjabi, Oriental, Indian)
Food- 3.00 | Meal per plate-₹850 onwards

Red Coral has been catering to parties of corporates for 20 years now. They will provide you a custom-made menu whether it is for 70 persons or 300. They specialize in Rajasthani, Mexican, Punjabi, Oriental and Indian cuisine. A veg platter costs ₹850 and a non-veggie ₹1000. An advance payment of upto 20 per cent and three to four days' notice are what they expect.

■ **City Square Mall, 3rd Floor, Near Raja Garden, Rajouri Garden, New Delhi, Ph: 9810994332**

Rahul Caterers & Decorators

Multi-Cuisine (Chinese, European, Indian, Italian, Mughlai) Noon to 11pm
Food-2.50. | Meal per plate-₹250

Rahul Caterers knows how much guests it can handle at one time with ease — not more than 200 in any case. Be it a birthday party or a family get-together or an anniversary they can cater Chinese, European, Indian, Italian, Mughlai, South cuisine and will work out a customized menu for you. So, they won't quote the price of a meal per plate. You have to make a down-payment of 10 per cent of the total money before you make your booking and a notice of five days is equally important. Rahul Caterers have been in business for the last 15 days.

■ **7703, Ram Nagar, Paharganj, New Delhi, Ph: 23549246, 9811177861**

Real Punjabi

Multi-Cuisine (Chinese, Mughlai)
Food- 2.50 | Meal per plate-₹100 onwards

Real Punjabi owner Jagmohan Singh has made all efforts to provide the real taste of Punjab. Real Punjabi makes Mughlai and Chinese cuisine. Punjabi Tawa Chicken is a speciality with this caterer. They have restricted themselves to catering for not more than 50 persons. Usually they cater to women's kitty parties, birthday parties, family get-together and anniversaries. You need to make a partial down-payment and make your booking in advance whatever you are engaging Real Punjabi for. They have catered to celebrities like Shankar Sawhney and Mika. Real Punjabi has been catering to people in Gurgaon for the six years.

■ **Shop No. 14, HUDA Market, Sector 23, Gurgaon, Ph: 9873154415, 9213675196, 9990320888**

Rizkquin Caterers

Indian, Mughlai
Food- 2.75 | Meal per plate-₹100 onwards

Salman Karhani, the proprieter of Rizkquin Caterers, can cater to any number of people, with a minimum of 50. For more than 15 years they have been providing food at parties for corporates and for weddings. They do both Indian and Mughalai cuisine. Korma, Biryani, White Gosht, Paneer Tikka and Chicken Tikka are some of the dishes that they specialize in. One week's notice and a 30 per cent advance payment are needed. You have to pay ₹100 for a veg platter and an extra ₹50 for a non-veg one.

■ **582, Sector 12, Near Sangam Cinema, RK Puram, New Delhi, Ph: 9818483237, 9268157222**

Sangam Tent & Caterers

Multi-Cuisine (Chinese, Indian, North Indian, South Indian, Chaat) 9.30am to 8pm
Food- 2.50 | Meal per plate-₹ 150 onwards

Those of you staying in the Rohini area of West Delhi can seek Sangam to cater for any of the function you might be holding at home — a small birthday party, an anniversary party or a big wedding reception. Sangam can take care of 50 to 4000 guests at a time. Chinese, Indian, North Indian, South Indian and Chaat are a speciality of this caterer who also operates a tent house. You have to give them a notice of one week and pay a minimum of 50 per cent of the total money as advance. Their meals cost a minimum of ₹150.

■ **F 2/73, Sector 16, Rohini, Delhi, Ph: 9312270379**

Salltt Catering

Multi-Cuisine (Chinese, European, French, Indian, Italian, Mexican)
Food- 3.00 | Meal per plate-₹1000 onwards

In the 15 years Salltt have been in business they have catered to celebrities like Kapil Dev, fashion designer JJ Vallya and model Amarpreet Wahi. They customize their menu according to their clients' tastes and you can have anything — Chinese, European, French, Indian, Italian, Mexican or multi-cuisine or even Thai cuisine. Whether you have as few guests as 25 guests or as many as 5,000, Salltt can handle them all with equal ease. They specialize in Mutton Nihari, Paneer Laang Latta, Lasange and Grilled Fish with Fresh Capers. If you happen to go to them, don't miss out on Boondi Rabadi. A vegetarian platter costs ₹1000 and a non-vegetarian one is priced at ₹1250.

■ **426, MG Road, Near Ghittorni Metro Station, Andheria More, Mehrauli, New Delhi, Ph: 9811035388**

Salt & Pepper

MULTI-CUISINE (Awadhi, Chinese, European, Goan, Indian, Italian, Kashmiri, Mughlai, Rajasthani, Pan-Indian, Oriental)

Food- 2.75 | Meal per plate-₹800 onwards

Akhil Sabharwal, who owns Salt & Pepper, has two things to boasts of — 25 years in the profession and catering to parties hosted by Bollywood celebrities in Delhi. If you are to host a big party — birthdays, anniversaries or weddings — you can have your pick from the variety of cuisines that Salt & Pepper makes: Awadhi, Chinese, European, Goan, Indian, Italian, Kashmiri, Mughlai, Rajasthani, Pan-Indian, Oriental. A veggie platter costs ₹800 and a non-vegetarian platter ₹1500. This caterer can provide for 100 to 3000 persons. When hosting a marriage party provide a notice of not less than six months. A down payment of 50 per cent is mandatory.

■ **J 13/18, Patel Market, Opp. HDFC Bank, Rajouri Garden, New Delhi, Ph: 25423400, 9810401230**

Saluja Caterers

MULTI-CUISINE (Chinese, European, Indian, Italian, Japanese, Mexican, Rajasthani, Thai) 9am to 9pm

Food- 2.50

For the last 10 years Saluja Caterers has been hosting large, upmarket and private functions like birthday parties, anniversaries, weddings. They can also provide food to parties held at offices or business workshops and seminars. Apart from all the cuisine that they offer they also prepare Punjabi, Oriental and Marwari delicacies. You can think of hiring Saluja for a party of as few as 50 guests to as many as 5000. But you need to inform them two days in advance. You have to pay 25 per cent of the total amount during booking, 50 per cent before the function and the rest after the function. Log on to www.salujacaterers.com for details on Saluja Caterers.

■ **11, DDA Flats, Shivalik, Panchsheel, Near Malviya Nagar, New Delhi, Ph: 9810789300, 9310789300**

■ **Sector 15, Naya Bans, Noida, Ph: 0120-2513228/9**

■ **RTF 53, Royal Tower Market, Shipra Suncity, Indirapuram, Ghaziabad**

Shrikrishan Maharaj

INDIAN - VEG (Marwari, Punjabi, Bengali, Gujarati) 24Hours

Food-3.00 | Meal per plate-₹350

If you are looking for someone who specializes in shakahari food, you could turn to Shrikrishan Maharaj, who makes home-made food away from home and delivers it at the doorstep. Maharaj's catering-service menu covers the entire gamut.

Marwari, Punjabi, Bengali, Gujarati delicacies... you name it, he cooks them all! Specially recommended is Dal Bati Churma, Undhiya, Thepla, Gujarati Kadhi and Dhokla. Do remember to order a week in advance, with a minimum order for 50 persons.

■ 53/2, Yusuf Sarai, New Delhi, Ph: 26196883, 26190496

Shubhangi

MULTI-CUISINE (Indian, Chinese, Thai, Tex-Mex, Italian, European)10am to 8pm
Food-2.75 | Meal per plate-₹400

Shukumar Mukherjee, in Noida, is an experienced caterer who has recently set up shop in the city. And with his offerings like Chinese, Thai, Italian, Indian, Tex-Mex and European, Sukumar doesn't disappoint. He is the person to turn to for regular stuff like Rogan Josh, Butter Chicken, Kadhai Chicken.... Even though he does provide Italian, Chinese, European and Thai dishes on request, it's really his Indian repertoire that he is better known for. Particularly popular is his Dum Aloo Achari which is somewhat of a house speciality. Catering to corporate events and weddings, Mukherjee requires a minimum 24-hour notice with a minimum order of 50.

■ B 5/12, Sector 31, Noida, Ph: 0120-4224277, 9811331191

Signature Cuisine

MULTI-CUISINE (Chinese, Indian, North Indian, Mughlai, European)
Food- 2.75 | Meal per plate-₹300 onwards

What makes Signature Cuisine unique is their claim to provide a signature dish from across India or abroad. They can supply Chinese, Indian, North Indian, Mughlai and European cuisine even while catering for up to 50 or 1000 persons. Allahabadi Gosht, Agra Chicken, Nihari Gosht and Butter Chicken are some of the cuisine that Signature boasts of. A veg platter costs ₹300 and a non-vegetarian one ₹500. Signature require three to 15 days' notice and an advance payment. They have been in the business for close to one year and it is mostly the corporates who are on their client list.

■ 320 A Block SK, Opp 82 Sec, Sec 110, Noida, Ph: 9891912488, 9818429786

SK Iyer Caterers

MULTI-CUISINE (Chinese, South Indian)
Food- 2.75 | Meal per plate-₹

From his house in one of the lanes off the Patparganj Road, S Krishnan runs his catering business. Whatever the occasion — birthday parties, family get-togethers, anniversaries, weddings, office parties, outdoor catering for religious functions or even if it is packed meals for groups travelling by train — you can bank upon Krishnan. He prepares North Indian, South Indian and Chinese cuisines but South Indian food is what Iyer makes best. He caters for 15 to 500 persons. If you have many people on your guest list you need to give one week's notice to SK Iyer Caterers. Deposit part of the money when you make your booking.

■ 226 A/B, Patparganj Road, Mayur Vihar, Phase 1, Delhi, Ph: 22758560. 9891077068

Sri Badrinath Caterers

MULTI-CUISINE/VEG (Chinese, European, North Indian, South Indian)
Food- 2.50

Whether your party has 50 guests or 10000 Sri Badrinath tries to live up to your expectations when it comes to catering. They cater to birthdays, anniversaries, weddings, office parties, seminars or workshops that your office might be thinking of organizing. Chinese, European, North Indian, South Indian cuisine is what they provide. Pasta, Macaroni and Salads are some of the dishes that you ask for when you opt for the European cuisine. The choice of menu is yours and they can provide you with several options. One to two days of notice is needed. You have to deposit 50 per cent of the total money as advance. They have been in the business for the last five years.

■ **1, Sector 14, Near Neelam Vihar Society, Kaushambi, Ghaziabad, Ph: 9868256086**

■ **11, LG Ground Floor, Indrapuram, Delhi, Ph: 986825086**

Subhash Tent House & Ankit Caterers

MULTI-CUISINE (Chinese, Indian, North Indian) 10am to 8pm
Food-2.50 | **Meal per plate-₹350 onwards**

For 20 years Sudan Gupta has been catering to all kinds of parties in the Sheikh Sarai area in South Delhi. The advantage of approaching him is that you don't have to run to a tent housewallah. They provide Chinese, Indian, North Indian cuisine but the choice of the menu will rest with you. A veg meal is priced at ₹350 and a Non-veg meal costs ₹450. Ankit Caterers will book orders for parties which has 100 or more guests. And they can cater for a maximum of 5000 persons. In any case they would need a notice of three days. Pay 20 per cent of the total amount in advance to ensure that things will run smooth.

■ **102 Pocket, Phase II, Near Super Bazaar, Sheikh Sarai, New Delhi, Ph: 29256616, 9810682829, 9871782424**

Subhi's Home Made

INDIAN (Punjabi, Sindhi) 9am to 9pm
Food- 3.00

Although known mainly for making finger-licking pickles, Subhi Ramchandani runs a catering service for the benefit of her friends, relatives and acquaintances. She prepares both veg and Non-veg food. Sindhi Curry, Gatte ki Curry and Palak Paneer are some of her veggie dishes. Among the non-veg items are Dum Pukht, Rogan Josh, Patrani Fish and Fish Curry. She makes many kinds of pickles, mostly Sindhi and Punjabi varieties. Mango grated with lemon and chick pea, and tomato chutney are hot favourites with regular customers. If Subhi has been catering to you for some time she will not ask for any money in advance but she does need a two-day notice. She has been in the business for almost six years.

■ **44, Sector 7, Near Kali Bari Mandir, RK Puram, New Delhi, Ph: 32560523, 9313439169**

Sukhbir Tent & Caterers

MULTI-CUISINE (Chinese, Indian, Mughlai)
Food- 2.50

Located on the Main Devli Road Sukhbir Tent & Caterers caters to people living around the Khanpur area. They prepare Chinese, Indian, and Mughlai cuisine. Be it a birthday party, anniversary, a large family get-together or wedding Sukhbir caters on all occasion with customized menu that would suit you. A three-day notice and a down payment of 30 per cent is needed to book your order. They can easily handle 100 to 2000 plus persons at a time. A veggie meal costs ₹400 and non-vegeterian ₹600. The have been in the profession for 40 years and have also catered for celebrities in the city.

F 98, Main Devni Road, Khanpur, Delhi, Ph: 9811276070

Sushi King

JAPANESE 11pm to 11.30pm
Food-3.50 | **Meal per plate-₹375**

Sushi Rocks? It's on a roll! Sushi King has upped the ante further — with state-of-the art operations offering perfectly-packed Sushi at your doorstep. The offerings — both vegetarian and non-vegetarian — are limited to Maki rolls and Nigiris — there are California Uramakis, Hasomakis, Nigiris... and yes, a rather forgettable offering of iffy Miso Soup, gratis! The vegetarian sushi — the Shitake Mushroom Sushi and the Carrot, Cucumber and Avacado Sushi are impressive. The Pickled Raddish Sushi, however, is entirely forgettable. It's the Seafood Nigiris that's worth trying — the Tuna, the Salmon, the Eel and the Shrimp, each is top-of-the-line. Go for it! All in all, is this Sushi King a real Raja? It's comparable with almost the best — and that's commendable in itself.

DLF Cybercity, Ground Floor, Tower 8 C, DLF Phase II, Gurgaon, Ph: 0124-4005000, 40060000

Sushiya

JAPANESE 10am to 10pm
Food- 3.00 | **Meal per plate-₹400**

Other than over a dozen Japanese restaurants which have sprouted in Delhi, bearing testimony to the strength of our Sushi sensibilities is Sushiya, an innovative experiment of home-delivery Sushi. And for the price you pay, this is a great VFM option as far as Sushi prices go. Sushiya's Sushi isn't the best Sushi available in this city. And the good news for shakaharis is that the Sushi kaleidoscope has been further embellished with a customized array of vegetarian options. While all options — both veggie and non-vegetarian — are limited to Maki Rolls and Nigiris, the Vegetarian Set 2, which consists of two Asparagus Rolls, four Avocado Rolls, two Cucumber Rolls and two Avocado with Fresh Papaya Rolls, is certainly worth a shot. Those who are Sushi connoisseurs the Non Vegetarian Set 6 — two Fresh Red Tuna Nigiris, two Smoked Salmon Nigiris, two Fresh Salmon Nigiris, two Sea Prawn Nigiris and two Squid Nigiris are worth trying. The Non Vegetarian Set 2 is so pocket-friendly and it's really a bargain. It comprises two Prawn Rolls, two Red Tuna Rolls, three Smoked Salmon Rolls, three Fresh Salmon Rolls. All in all, it's all in the Sets.

B 113, Freedom Fighter Enclave, Main Ignou Road, Neb Sarai, New Delhi, Ph: 9310236466, 9312444086

Swagatam Caterers

Multi-Cuisine (Chinese, European, Indian) 8am to 6pm
Food- 2.50 | Meal per plate-₹700 onwards

Swagatam has catered to corporate houses and wedding parties only. They prepare Chinese, European, Indian cuisine. Chilli Manchurian, Chilli Paneer, Noodles (Veg/Non-veg), Hakka Noodles are some of the Chinese dishes that they prepare. A veggie platter costs ₹700 and a non-vegetarian platter ₹900. Swagatam caters to 100 to 2000 persons at a time. You need to deposit 25 per cent of the total money as advance and book your order at least three days prior to the party. They accept credit cards and have been catering in the Vasant Kunj area for 12 years.

■ 34/9, Kishangarh, Near City Bazaar, Vasant Kunj, Ph: 32594500, 9810186345

Swaran Caterers

Indian/Veg 11am to 4pm, 7pm to 11pm
Food- 2.50

If a small vegetarian get-together or a party is what you have on mind ask Swaran to cater. They can comfortably do so for 20 persons. You need to provide a notice of two days and an advance payment of at least 25 per cent of the total money. Swaran caters to people living in the Mansarovar Garden area.

■ F 23, Shopping Complex, Mansarovar Garden, Delhi, Ph: 64722752

Taneja Caterers & Decorators

Multi-Cuisine (Chinese, Indian, Italian, Mughlai) 9am to 9pm
Food- 2.50

Deepak Taneja runs catering service in Ramesh Nagar which prepares Chinese, Indian, Italian, Mughlai cuisine. They cater both vegetarian as well as non-vegetarian meals. Taneja Caterers can cater 100 to 1500 persons at a time. But you need to provide them a notice of two days. Call them for details. They have been catering for 35 years.

■ 4 /113 Ramesh Nagar, Near Gurdwara Singh Sabha, Ph: 25428898, 9810498202

Top Food & Beverage Catering Services

Multi-Cuisine (Chinese, European, Italain, Mexican, Thai)
Food- 3.00 | Meal per plate-₹1000 onwards

Amit Dua is hailed as a high-class caterer by his clients for the innovations that he has introduced in his preparations as also for the way he displays his buffet, fruit mocktail spread and bar counters. He serves multi-cuisine, and some of his specialties are Caramelized Onion, Beer Batter King Prawns, Cocktail Bhelpuri Tarts, Exotic Platter Hummus with Crack, Californian Grapes, Crispy Spinach Filo Basket, Smoked Chicken and Teriyaki Chicken. He is known most of all for his European cuisine. Backed up by a good team, Amit handles events like birthday parties to wedding feasts very well. The bigger the event the higher advance you need to pay. Top Food & Beverage caters 100 to 2000 persons. A vegetarian plate order costs between ₹1000 to ₹1200 and a non-vegetarian one ₹1200 to ₹1500. Three days' notice and an advance payment of 50 per cent are required to book your order. Amit has been running his business for four years. You can also visit his website *www.topfoods.in.*

G 23, Vardman Plaza City II, Asaf Ali Road, Ph: 23234639, 9990989100, 9990121100, 9810345424

United Catering Services

Multi-Cuisine (Chinese, European, Indian, Iranian, Italian, Mexican, Thai) 10am to 110pm

Food- 2.75| Meal per plate-₹550 Onwads

Akash Kumar Kalra, who owns United Catering Services, can cater to any number of guests. He has an experience of six years and provides customized menu to his clients. Akash specializes in European delicacies but also has the capability of doing Lebanese cuisine, Mongolian Chicken and Mexican dishes besides of course Indian. A vegetarian meal costs ₹550 while a non-vegetarian plate costs ₹700. You need to provide a notice of two days to almost a week if your requirement is large. Pay 25 per cent of the total amount as advance payment. They cater on birthdays, anniversaries, weddings and also for corporate houses. Akash comes from a family which has been supplying multi-cuisine food to big corporates, VIPs and private parties since 1942. Akash is capable of handling between 50 and 5000 persons.

29, Central Market, Punjabi Bagh, New Delhi, Ph: 66358786

Urban Kitchen, The

Multi-Cuisine (Chinese, European, Indian, Italian, Mexican, Thai) 9am to 6pm

Food- 2.50

Mira Jhalha runs her catering service from Sushant Lok in Gurgaon for two years now. Be it a big party or a wedding or a function of a corporate house, they will take care of the food. Although European cuisine a speciality she also makes delicacies from Chinese, European, Indian, Italian, Mexican, Thai cuisine. Mira can cater upto 5000 persons with the condition that you pay her 50 per cent of the money in advance.

LG 31-32 E, Sushant Shopping Arcade, Phase I, Gurgaon, Ph: 9650463210, 9910220632

Victory Caterers & Decoraters

Multi-Cuisine (Chinese, European, Indian, Mughlai, Thai) 10am to 8pm

Food- 2.50

Victory was established 50 years ago and caters to people in the Delhi Cantonment area. Whether it is a birthday party, anniversary, wedding or a large get-together you can rely on them. They make Chinese, European, Indian, Mughlai and Thai cuisine. Victory can cater upto 400 persons at a time. A deposit of 25 per cent is mandatory before booking an order and four days' notice is also required.

Gopinath Bazaar, Delhi Cantonment, Delhi, Ph: 25692060, 25693388

XO Catering Services

Multi-Cuisine (Indian, Chinese, Japanese, Thai, European) 24 hours

Food-3.75 | **Meal per plate-₹1000**

The venture of the talented Arjun Puri, this catering service has no single speciality but can turn out every cuisine from Greek and Lebanese to Thai and Japanese to Indian from virtually every region. Whether it is Goan, Rajasthani or Lucknavi, you can have the option of having a banquet at a wedding or a corporate event with a multiplicity of cuisines, in which at least six dishes will represent one cuisine. XO Catering Services puts together the best of the best and brings in the dining out experience for you. He offers a variety of cuisines, cutlery and waiter service including white gloved service, and requires 24-hour notice and a minimum order for 20 persons. Do order the Lamb Chops with Rosemary Jus, the Chicken Stuffed with Morels and Goat Cheese and the Grilled Fish with an Onion and Tomato Chutney — signature dishes that make him a master of the catering business.

■ **C 102 Chattarpur Enclave, New Delhi,**
Ph: 41600650, 9811283973

Zahid Catering Services

Mughlai

Food-3.50 | **Meal per plate-₹300**

Probably the finest biryani in the city today, Zahid is a master of all the dishes that he rustles up. Located in an inconvenient part of Delhi, he delivers to an address in Khan Market from where you have to pick up the supplies. His lamb biryani is highly recommended, followed by chicken biryani. Afghan chicken is expressly for those who appreciate subtle, non-spicy tastes and he does a variety of chicken tikkas with basic variations; none, however, with the same flair as the mind-blowing biryani. Book your order five to six days in advance. Zahid takes orders for not more than 50 persons at a time.

Ph: 9213165147

TIFFIN

A One Tiffin Service

Lunch 11.30am to 2pm

Meenu Khanna who owns A One has been running the tiffin service to provide meals for working men and women. Her meals are priced at ₹45 and ₹60 and the difference is that in the latter you get Paneer Subzi and a sweet. If you happen to stay in the range of 4 to 5km from her home you can have the food delivered at home free of cost. You need to place your order half an hour before. A One provides only vegetarian meals.

A 624, Sarita Vihar, New Delhi, Ph: 9268130003, 9999965312

Friction Entertainment

Lunch 12.30pm to 2pm, Dinner 7.30pm to 10.30pm

Notwithstanding its bizarre name, Friction Entertainment offers meals which remind you of home-cooked food. It serves clientele made up mostly of working men and women and students living in and around Sector 20 of Noida. The veg meal, which costs ₹40, comprises three chapatis, subzi with gravy, *sukhi subzi*, plain rice, *raita* and salad. The non-veg meal at ₹80 comes with three chapatis, two pieces of chicken with gravy, *sukhi* subzi, rice and salad. The ₹60 non-veg meal comprises three chapatis, egg bhurji or egg curry, *sukhi* subzi, rice, and salad. If you are sweet-toothed you can have sweets but you have to pay extra. Friction Entertainment delivers food at home free of charge.

A 30, Sector 20, Noida, Ph: 9871770267

Ghar Ka Khana Tiffin Services

Lunch 11am to 2pm, Dinner 6pm to 9pm

Ghar Ka Khana Tiffin Services, which offers meals to working people, operates from a home behind Kendriya Vihar in Noida. Serve as this outfit does wholesome and hygienically prepared food, it lives up to its name. Taking note of the growing distaste for spicy food, Ghar Ka Khana people use oil and masala sparingly. A meal comprising four chapatis, rice, *subzi*, dal and salad is priced at ₹40. A luxury meal, consisting of either two Lachcha Parantha or plain paranthas, rice, *raita,* sweets, dry *subzi* and *subzi* with curry, salad and pickle, costs ₹70. But they give only vegetarian food. Home delivery to those living nearby is free.

Behind Kendriya Vihar, Noida, Ph: 9891068519

Grandma's Kitchen Tiffin Service

Breakfast 7.30am to 10.30am, Lunch Noon to 3pm, Dinner 8pm to 11.30pm

Rachel Arora, who runs Grandma's Kitchen, loves to cook for her customers. No wonder her meals have the aroma of food prepared by your loved ones back home. Her meals are not only hygienic and tasty but also full of nutritional value. From her home at Vasundhara in Ghaziabad she sends packed meals (breakfast, lunch and dinner) to working men and women and students. She can even send lunch to your office if you work near her home. She prepares both veg and non-veg meals. Her breakfast for ₹45 has parantha with curd, Aloo

Puri, sandwiches and cup cakes. You will get milk on alternate days and egg twice a week. A vegetarian lunch or dinner at ₹50 has four chapatis or two paranthas, plain rice or fried rice, dal or one *subzi* with gravy and salad. For a non-veg meal, costing ₹75, you can choose from any of these — Egg Curry, Chicken Korma, Chicken Curry, Fish with gravy along with chapatis, rice, etc. Rachel provides all the meals in microwave-proof boxes. Her USA Foodie Friday Special gives the option of ordering regional cuisine — South Indian, Gujarati, Punjabi and Bengali. She also delivers her meals free in your home or office.

■ **Sector 5, Vasundhara, Near Vasundhara Plaza, Ghaziabad, Ph: 9711287992**

Himalayan Tiffin Service

Lunch 12.30pm, Dinner 7.30pm

Himalayan is a small-time tiffin service catering to people in the Rajendra Nagar area. Mostly working men and women opt for their services. They prepare their food at home and have been supplying it for the last eight years. Priced at ₹35, a meal consists of four chapatis, dal, *subzi* and rice.

■ **53/18, Rajendra Nagar, New Delhi, Ph: 25735559**

Home Made

Lunch 12.30pm to 2.30pm, Dinner 8.30pm to 10pm

For seven years Sanju Tandon has been providing lunch and dinner to offices, working men and women at Faridabad. They provide free home delivery in the range of 10km. Her meals cost ₹50 and comprises four chapatis, two subzis, salad, rice, and sweets once a week. A deluxe tiffin priced at ₹90 has four chapatis, two *subzis,* salad, rice, and sweets and the one which costs ₹110 consists of four chapatis, special paneer *subzi, sukhi subzi*, dal, curd, salad, rice and sweets. If you are ordering for the first time place your order an hour before you want the meal.

■ **2251, Near Mother Dairy, Sector 55, Faridabad, Ph: 9810169571, 9810427082**

Jain Food

Breakfast 8am to 10am, Lunch Noon to 3pm, Dinner 7.30pm to 9pm

Jain Food offer veg meals to people who want to avoid the drudgery of cooking or simply do not have the time for it. Predictable their fare may be but it is hygienic and palatable to the taste buds. Another point in Jain Food's favour is that they use minimum oil and spices. The breakfast comprising two paranthas along with dahi costs ₹40. Lunch and dinner are priced at ₹50 each. The meals consist of four chapatis, rice, dal, two *subzis* and a salad. Home delivery is free to those living in the Nehru Place, Kalkaji, Greater Kailash, Kailash Colony, Sant Nagar and Govind Puri areas.

■ **K22 A, 1st Floor, Kalkaji, New Delhi, Ph: 9313845860**

Krishna Food Plaza

Lunch Noon to 1pm, Dinner 7pm to 10pm

There is of course no substitute for the food your mom or your wife cooks at home. But if you work or study in Delhi or live here for any other reason, you do crave from time to time for home-cooked meals. Krishna claims to give you just that kind of food. The grub is hygienically cooked, tastes good and is reasonably priced. A lunch or a dinner comprising four chapatis, rice, dal, and one *subzi* costs ₹40, and is home-delivered free within a range of 2 to 3 km.

■ Shop No. 9, NDM Tower I, Netaji Subhash Place, New Delhi, Ph: 47508576, 08802083544

Lavnya Services

Breakfast 7.30am to 9am, Lunch Noon to 1pm, Dinner 7.30pm to 8pm

Lavnya provide breakfast, lunch and dinner to working men and women and students who are reluctant to cook or eat out. If you live within 3km from Lavnya you can have your meals delivered to your home free of charge. The breakfast is for ₹50 and comprises one *subzi,* two paranthas, *dahi* and *achar*. And the fare for lunch and dinner is four chapatis, two *subzis,* rice and salad, and is priced at ₹60 each. Lavnya have been catering to people for the last one year.

■ 17/514, DDA Flat, Kalkaji, New Delhi, Ph: 69501193, 9910616625

Laxmi Kitchen

Lunch 11.30am to 2pm, Dinner 7pm to 9pm

If you live in Sector 19 of Noida and are trying to find out who could deliver meals to you at your home everyday contact Laxmi Kitchen. They provide veg meals to working men and women. The food is both hygienic and wholesome. Their lunch, priced at ₹40, consists of four chapatis, rice, dal, subzi and salad. The dinner, which costs ₹70, comprises four chapatis, Paneer Subzi, *subzi,* rice, curd and sweets. If you want to have a special dish you can order it two hours in advance. Home delivery is free for those who live in the vicinity of Laxmi Kitchen.

■ B 50, 2nd Floor, Sector 19, Near Post Office, Noida, Ph: 9650573152, 9990114065

Man Pasand Tiffin Service

Lunch Noon to 2pm, Dinner 7pm to 9pm

It might not be your *man pasand* place to order meals but you will not dislike the food that they dish out. Man Pasand Tiffin Service tries hard to live up to its name with smart chefs making wholesome food. They deserve praise for being hygienic and for using oil and spices sparingly. The meals come in two categories — four chapatis, dal, rice, subzi and salad cost ₹40 if you are a regular customer. The same meal will cost you ₹45 if you are not a regular customer. They even provide breakfast which is comprised of two paranthas and pickles and is priced at ₹20.

■ E 5/11, 3rd Floor, Near Rimpy Restaurant, Malviya Nagar, New Delhi, Ph: 9971944858, 9811045666, 9818250206

Mess, The

Lunch 12.30pm 2.30pm, Dinner 7.30pm to 10.30pm

The Mess owner Nishit Singh has devised a novel strategy to lure customers. He offers discount on his meals if you pay him money for a month in advance. That apart, he delivers food in the radius of 5km from The Mess. A meal costs ₹35 and consists of four chapatis, *subzi*, dal, rice, salad and chutney. A luxury meal at ₹50 comprises four chapatis or two paranthas, Paneer Subzi, dal, Mattar Rice or Zeera Rice, *raita* and sweets. Nishit's Sunday Special at ₹60 comes with *puri, kheer* or *halwa* and Chhole Bhature. But on Sunday evening you have to eat elsewhere because The Mess is closed for dinner.

■ **Near Labour Chowk, Sector 58, Noida, Ph: 0120-6491390, 9212442970**

Om Tiffin Services — Pure Veg Ghar ki Rasoi Se

Lunch Noon to 1.30pm, Dinner 7.30pm to 8.30pm

Om Tiffin Services has employed experienced chefs to prepare homemade food which they pack in Tiffins for working men and women, university students, etc. The meal costs ₹50 for four chapatis, rice, *subzi* salad, pickle and ₹60 for adding Paneer Subzi to the ₹50 meal. Only those availing meal services regularly can get free home delivery. Even the bulk orders are delivered free.

■ **B 39, Nanda Road, Adarsh Nagar, Delhi, Ph: 9312053626, 9999401607, 9971495101**

Panditji Hot Tiffin & Caterers

Lunch Noon to 3pm, Dinner 7pm to 9.30pm

Panditji provides lunch and dinner to working people who find it hard to cook at home for want of time. The tiffin service he owns provides homemade food. There are two types of tiffin — one which consists of four chapatis, *subzi,* dal, rice and salad for ₹40. The deluxe tiffin has Paneer Subzi, dal, four chapatis, rice, salad and sweet for ₹60. But they also operate as caterer and prepare good food with the expert chefs they have employed. Since they cater to parties also they make veg-only grub — Indian, South Indian, Chinese, Fruit Juice, etc. Needless to say, Panditji offers free home-delivery.

■ **56, IP Extn, Hasanpur, Patparganj, Delhi, Ph: 43055855, 9811313080, 9873666580**

Pankaj Tiffin's

Lunch 12.30pm to 2pm, Dinner 7pm to 9.30pm

Pankaj has employed experienced cooks who make wholesome meals for people staying as paying guests, working men and women, and students staying in the NCR region of Gurgaon. For ₹45 you can have four chapatis, dal, *subzi,* rice, and salad. Four chapatis, dal, *subzi,* rice, salad, sweets and curd make the special tiffin which costs ₹65. Their buffet meal is for ₹65 and provides unlimited food but that has to be ordered for 50 people.

■ **Sector 7, Gurgaon, Ph: 9999359339**

Punjabi Rasoi

Lunch 11am to 2pm, Dinner 6pm to 8pm

From her home in Kalkaji, Ritu caters to offices in Kalkaji and Okhla. She packs homemade meals in tiffins and gets them delivered to people free of cost in their offices. A meal of four chapatis, dal, *raita, subzi,* rice and salad costs ₹65. Punjabi

Rasoi refrains from using too much oil and spices to make the food appear as if it has been prepared at home.

■ **154, 2nd Floor, Kalkaji, New Delhi, Ph: 8860755989**

Rekha Bhatia Tiffin Service

Lunch 11.30am, Dinner 6.30pm

Rekha provides hygienic food which tastes like homemade food. She has employed experienced cooks who use oil sparingly and little of spices. The meal you get for ₹40 has four chapatis, dal, *subzi,* rice, and once a week, Paneer Subzi. You can have *raita,* a sweet dish each at an additional cost of ₹10. You can have the privilege of free home delivery only if you live in Vikas Puri. Rekha Bhatia supplies meals to office, individuals who live as paying guests, and working men and women.

■ **AG 1/123 B, Vikas Puri, New Delhi, Ph: 25525792, 9811815583**

Reshma's Tiffin

Lunch Noon to 2pm, Dinner 7pm to 9pm

Paying guests, working men and women, small parties and lunches at offices is what Reshma's caters to from her home in Vasant Kunj. There are two different rates for the meals that you get from her. For the tiffin with three chapatis, dal, *subzi,* rice, salad, *papad* and pickles you have to pay ₹50. The special meal costs ₹70 and comprises three chapatis, dal, *subzi,* rice, salad, papad, pickle, raita and dessert. Reshma has been running the tiffin service for the last 14 years.

■ **90, Sector C, Vasant Kunj, New Delhi, Ph: 26122521, 26896701, 9810290222**

Sai Tiffin Services

Lunch Noon to 2pm, Dinner 7pm to 10pm

Sai Tiffin prepares homemade food in a clean environment using all the ingredients that they make in-house. They prepare meals for students, and working men and women who find it difficult to cook at home. For ₹45 you will get value-for-money food which comprises Paneer Subzi thrice a week. Normal tiffin costs ₹45 and has four chapatis, dal, salad, *subzi* and rice. Those who order their meals from Sai Tiffin on a regular basis swear by the fresh food that they serve. Even those who wish to order for meal once in a blue moon have the option of ordering in advance (lunch 10am and dinner 4pm). Free home delivery can be availed of only by those living in Rohini. For Pitampura they charge ₹10 per tiffin.

■ **B 15, Overseas Apartment, Opp. Sector 9, Telephone Exchange, Rohini, Delhi, Ph: 66362803, 9999775965**

Tiffin Services

Saranjeet Singh, the owner of Tiffin Services, has worked as a chef in a five-star hotel in Punjab and cashes in on this experience to run this service. He provides only veggie food to people living in Tilak Nagar area. For the last three years he has been supplying meals to students and working men and women. He gets the meals prepared at home. His tiffin comprises one dal, four chapatis, *subzi,* and rice and costs ₹35.

Free home delivery is available to regular customers in the nearby areas. You have to pay ₹40 per tiffin after the 6km range.

M 52, Ground Floor, Near Gurudwara Singh Sabha, Street No. 5, Tilak Nagar, New Delhi, Ph: 25997580, 9717846535

Traffic Jam Caterers

Lunch 11.30am to 4pm, Dinner 7.30pm to 9.30pm

Traffic Jam Caterers cash in on using good ingredients that make the meals wholesome. And there is a kind of fan following among bachelors in this locality for the food that they serve as meals. This tiffin service is known for the Basmati rice it uses. The lunch comprises four chapatis, rice, dal one subzi and costs ₹50, and the dinner is priced at ₹65 and has four chapatis, rice, dal, one subzi, sweets and salad. If you live within 3 to 4 km of Traffic Jam Caterers you can have your meals delivered at your doorstep free of cost.

SD 154, Tower Apartment, Pitampura, Delhi, Ph: 9818224270

Yashasvi Tiffin Service

Lunch Noon, Dinner 8pm

Yashasvi prepares wholesome meals for students, working men and women. They make vegetarian-only meals which are much like homemade food. For ₹50 you can get four chapatis, rice, dal, salad, *subzi* once a week and, paneer. At Yashasvi oil and masalas are used sparingly so that people who eat regularly don't complain of stomach ailments.

RZ I61, Mahavir Enclave, New Delhi, Ph: 9911919736

COOKING CLASSES

Aarti Aggarwal

CHOCOLATES, ICE CREAMS, MOCKTAILS, EGGLESS CAKES, MULTI-CUISINE

Aarti Aggarwal's motto is easy, healthy, and delicious cooking, because, according to her, this is what everyone wants these days. Her recipes are not only easy to master but also nutritious, for example her non-fried dishes. She offers courses in breakfast, starters, kebabs, sizzlers, Chinese, Italian, Lebanese, Mexican and Thai, and you can join any of these. She also gives lessons in making chocolates, ice creams, mocktails, eggless cakes, etc. The timings for Aarti Aggarwal's classes are: 11am to 1.30pm, 4pm to 6.30pm, Monday to Saturday. You can find out more about her classes and culinary skills by logging on to *www.aartiaggarwal.com.*

▪ 5/200, Ground Floor, Sunder Vihar, Paschim Vihar, New Delhi, Ph: 9810475569, 25269063

Batra Cooking Institute

COOKERY CLASSES

Those of you who are enterprising and wish to run catering services for tiffins, kitty parties or birthday parties can join Batra classes to learn how to make dishes for these events. Batra gives lessons to students at her home in batches of 30 to 40 and 20 to 25. The timings are: 9.30am to 11.30am. The Batra Cooking Institute has been running classes in Delhi for the last 15 years.

▪ C 153, Vikas Puri, New Delhi, Ph: 9810058239, 25507151

Chef Culinaire, The

DESSERTS, CAKES, CHINESE, ITALIAN, JAPANESE, LEBANESE, MEXICAN, SOUTH INDIAN, THAI

Manju Monga has been teaching culinary skills for 11 years. On CNBC Awaz and ETV she comes up with her own recipes for dishes she specializes in. Griha Laxmi too has carried her recipes. Manju has specialized in low-calorie dishes which she has incorporated into Chinese, Italian, Japanese, Lebanese, Mexican, South Indian and Thai cuisine, and this is also what she teaches in her cookery classes. At her desserts and cakes demonstration classes her students gain hands-on training. She also makes a variety of kebabs and sandwiches. The classes are held in two sessions: 11am to 2pm and 4pm to 7pm. Manju's website *http://www.manjumonga.com* tells us in details about her expertise and classes.

▪ A 97, Gujranwala Town, Part I, Delhi, Ph: 9810894741, 9213559761

Culinary & Cake Decorating School

FAR EASTERN, EUROPEAN, MIDDLE EASTERN, PARISIAN SUGAR CRAFTING, CONFECTIONERY

At the Culinary & Cake Decorating School (CCDS) you will find serious learners who swear by the culinary skills they learn there. CCDS offers courses in Far Eastern cuisines, European food, Parisian cooking, Back-to-the-basics Western Cuisine,

Indian, Desserts & Chocolates, Baking 101, Indian Sweets, Middle-Eastern cuisine, Children's Party Favourites, Napkin Folding, Specialty Skilled Courses, Sugar Craft & String Work and Confectionery. Cake Day Workshops are also held. The classes are held from Monday to Friday between 9.30am and 6.30pm. The timings for the classes on Saturdays and Sundays are 11am to 4pm.

■ **New Friends Colony, The Suryaa, New Delhi, Ph: 46323679**

Dimpi Cookery Classes

CHINESE, EUROPEAN, ICE CREAMS, PUDDINGS, CAKES

Gurdeep Kaur offers classes in Chinese, European, North Indian and South Indian delicacies. What she specializes in is ice creams, puddings and cakes, and you can learn a variety of them if you join her classes. Dimpi charges ₹200 to teach how to prepare one single dish. Usually the courses run for three months. She has been teaching cookery for four years.

■ **G 58, Ist Floor, Lane No. 11, G Block, Near Jail Road, Near Janakpuri, Shiv Nagar, New Delhi, Ph: 9811224428**

Kanchan Cookery Classes

ICE CREAMS, DESSERTS, NORTH INDIAN

Kanchan has been giving cookery classes for 10 years. She specializes in desserts and ice creams, of which she will teach you many varieties. She offers to make you an expert in North Indian cuisine. She has short-term courses too — usually lasting 10 days — where she teaches no less than 25 to 30 dishes. And you will have to pay something between ₹2500 to ₹4000 for a 10-day course. But once you have taken her 10-day course you will cook with confidence and win a lot of appreciation too. This is what Kanchan promises.

■ **Ph: 9910197736**

Khadyam Cooking Academy

CAKES, ITALIAN, LEBANESE, MEXICAN, THAI

Leena Aghi, the trainer at Khadyam, has devised two different types of courses for those coming to her cookery classes — a day-long course for fast learners and a seven- to eight-day course for those slow on the uptake. Italian, Lebanese, Mexican and Thai cuisines are what she teaches. She also gives lessons in making soups, salads and sizzlers and offers courses in baking cakes and making chocolates. Khadyam's classes have been running in Delhi for a little more than three years now.

■ **Ph: 9999377415, 9212283404**

Lifelong Learning

CHINESE, ITALIAN, MUGHLAI, SOUTH INDIAN, MOCKTAILS, DESSERTS

Among the many courses that Lifelong Learning offers only to women cookery is one. It teaches how to prepare food from scratch — cutting, chopping, preparing spices, yoghurt, etc. The classes give lessons on making breakfast, lunch, dinner and snacks. The next level takes up multi-cuisine where you get to learn Chinese, Italian, Mughlai, and South Indian cuisine and also how to make mocktails and desserts. They put as much emphasis on presentation of a dish as preparing it. The classes are held three days a week and for two hours a day — from 11am to 1pm, 2pm to 4pm or 3pm to 5pm. Working women can opt for the weekend batches for any of these courses. There is no age for women attending cookery classes. Log on to *www.lifelonglearning.in* for details on the courses offered.

M 3, South Extn. Part II, Ring Road, New Delhi, Ph: 9717293748/50/51

A 34, 2nd Floor, Ring Road, Rajouri Garden, Next to Rajouri Flyover, New Delhi, Ph: 45134444

Madhu Gupta Cooking Classes

Mughlai, Chinese, Mexican, Cakes, Ice Creams, Mocktails

Madhu Gupta is a housewife who has morphed into a professional cook. She began teaching cookery after her daughter got married and her sons left home to study elsewhere. Madhu specializes in cooking Mughlai, Chinese, and Mexican cuisines and gives lessons in making cakes, ice creams, chocolates, mocktails, puddings, salads with vegetable carving, baked snacks, cookies and biscuits, Danish pastries, low-fat cooking, microwave cooking and cooking for first-timers. She has a website which posts recipes on making chaat, Chinese cuisine, chocolates, fried snacks, ice cream, Mexican food, Mughlai, puddings, etc. She is popular among students because her food is tasty and she uses ingredients available at her home. Log on to *http://www.madhugupta.com* to know more about her classes.

16, Bungalow Road, Kamla Nagar, Delhi, Ph: 23843675, 9968053589

Neeta Khurana's Classes

Ice Creams, Chocolates, Cakes, Indian, European, Oriental

Having taught cookery for nine years, Neeta is as particular about making dal, the simplest of Indian dishes, as she is about making the most exquisite cakes like the Fresh Pineapple Upside Down Cake and the Chocolate Truffle. She herself takes the classes in batches of four to six people. Neeta also teaches cooking to people coming from abroad. She gives lessons in Baking, Indian Cuisine, European Cuisine, Oriental Cuisine, Ice Creams and Chocolates. That apart, she also takes orders for weddings, parties and get-togethers during festivals. The duration of her courses varies from just a day to two days or a little more. Visit her website *http://neetakhurana.com* for timings, course fees and other details.

E 179, Kalkaji, New Delhi, Ph: 41601458, 9810080584

Nita Mehta

Chocolates, Chinese, Indian, Italian, Lebanese, Mexican, Salads

The winner of the Best Asian Cookbook Award in Paris in 1999 and a Delhi University home science graduate, Nita Mehta's books on cookery can be found in both big cities and small towns across India. She has also appeared in several cookery programmes on TV channels. Nita gives classes in chocolate-making and Chinese, Indian, Italian, Lebanese, Mexican cuisine as also in making salads, sizzlers and a variety of sandwiches. The classes are conducted across Delhi and the NCR region — Central Delhi, West Delhi, South Delhi, Gurgaon and Noida. The classes are held for three hours —

from 10.30am to 1.30pm. The fee starts from ₹900 and varies from course to course. You can log on to *www.nitamehta.com* to know more about her and her classes.

■ **Ph: 23252948, 23250091**

Perfect Cookery

CHOCOLATES, CAKES, BROWNIES, INDIAN, CHINESE, EUROPEAN

Those living in Greater Kailash and the NCR region of Gurgaon and Noida can take lessons in cooking from Ramni Ralhan. There are short-term courses which teach you how to make chocolates and cakes as also cookies and brownies. The courses she imparts on Indian, Chinese and European cuisine promise to help you master these dishes. Classes are held six days a week. The timings are: 11am to 1pm and 3pm to 8pm. After you are through with the courses you can notice what it does to you — the appreciation you get at home or from friends and relatives invited to your home for lunch or dinner. Log on to *http://ramniralhan.com* for details on Ramni and her classes.

■ **M 28, Main Market, Greater Kailash Part I, New Delhi**

■ **A 89, Sector 41, Noida**

■ **C 632, Sushant Lok 1, Gurgaon, Ph: 9312507387, 9810515445, 9899286764**

Rano Suri

CAKES, CHINESE, ITALIAN, MEXICAN, SOUTH INDIAN

Rano Suri has been giving cookery lessons for 10 years. She has also given demonstrations on microwave cooking for BPL for six years, and for VLCC on how low-calorie food can be prepared. She has written three books and her column on recipes has appeared in magazines like *Femina* and *Savvy*. You can learn to prepare Chinese, Italian, Mexican, and South Indian dishes. Besides, she knows the art of making a variety of snacks which she teaches her students. She also holds classes on cake-making. Her courses last from four to 20 days. Call her to find out about the timings and the course fees.

■ **C 139, Kirti Nagar, New Delhi, Ph: 9810650019, 9891749400**

Rupali's Cookery

CAKES, DESSERTS, SOUPS, SALADS CHINESE, ITALIAN, MEXICAN, MUGHLAI, THAI

Rupali's popularity has soared ever since she began hosting the cookery show *Aks-e-Rasoi* on ETV Urdu channel. She offers different types of courses which range from making cakes and desserts to soups, salads, and barbeque. That apart, she gives her students lessons in preparing Chinese, Italian, Mexican, Mughlai and Thai cuisines. Rupali's classes are held in fully-equipped modern kitchens and each session lasts two -and-a-half hours — 11am to 1.30pm. Her courses are usually short — one to two days.

■ **C 632, Sushant Lok I, Gurgaon, Ph: 9899286764, 0124-2577264**

Smell & Taste

ICE CREAM, CAKES, ITALIAN, MEXICAN, SOUTH INDIAN

Apart from multi-cuisine recipes, Meenakshi offers lessons in bakery items and chocolates. While her short-term courses last for three days, the duration of long-term courses is 10 days. She also holds baking, Chinese cookery, chocolate-making, European cooking, ice cream-making, Italian cooking, Mexican cooking, South Indian cooking and sweets-making classes. Meenakshi has been conducting classes for 10 years and also running three-month certificate courses. The timings for the classes are 11am to 1pm and 4pm to 6pm. Visit the website *http://prepup.indobase.com* for details.

218, Star Apartment, Sector 9, Rohini, Delhi, Ph: 9810216232

Sugarcraft Classes

Cakes, Decoration

Swati Jain, who generally makes exclusive celebration cakes, is also into sugar craft which she uses for creating various designs on the delicacies that she makes. Every three to four months Sugarcraft holds workshops all over India. The cake varieties she makes are: Doll Cakes, Chocolate Cakes, Cup Cakes, Floral Delight, Fairy House and Choco Floral Ecstasy. These workshops are self-contained with all the tools, ingredients, techniques and recipes available in-house. That apart, Sugarcraft gives live instructions and provides Web-support. Log on to *http://sugarcraftindia.wordpress.com* to know more details about Swati's classes. You can send email to Swati at *sugarcraftindia@gmail.com.*

09800093323

Taruna Aggarwal Cookery Classes

Cakes, Chinese, Snacks, Puddings, Mocktails, Salads

After Taruna Aggarwal thought of giving cookery classes, invitations to ladies' club in-house programmes came pouring in. From cakes to Chinese, snacks to puddings, and mocktails to salads, she has perfection in a variety of cuisines. She has been to the Dale Carnegie Institute of Public Speaking, USA and this is quite obvious when she conducts her classes. Visit Taruna's website: *http://tarunaaggarwal.com* for details about her classes.

9F, Kamla Nagar, Opp. Bada Gol Chakkar, Delhi

E 502, Greater Kailash II, New Delhi, Ph: 9717048000, 9811591348

Vreehi Food Academy

Arabian, Chinese, European, Indian, Multi-Cuisine, Thai Pastry, Cakes

Chef Aman Kumar, who has worked with Burj Al Arab and was also selected for Celebrity Cruises (in the USA), formed a team to offer practical training in all cuisines. Vreehi, the food academy, promises to make you a thorough professional who can begin his/her own project in culinary arts, baking, pastry arts and food service management. It teaches a wide range of multi-national cuisines in a very short time. The cuisines include Indian, European, Thai, Arabian, Pastry, etc. Their six + three-month crash course enables the students to get hands-on training in a five-star hotel. Their one-and-a-half year diploma course promises job with hotels and cruise line in the USA and other countries. Visit their website *http://www.vreehi.com* for details.

C 352, Ramphal Chowk, Palam Extn, Sector 7, Dwarka, New Delhi, Ph: 25074565, 9968073404

INGREDIENTS

A T Exims

9.30am to 6pm

375 B, DDA Flats, Gazipur, New Delhi, Ph: 22731839, 22777227

Oils: Chilli Oil (Thai), Extra Virgin Olive, Virgin Olive, Pure Olive, Pomace Olive.

Food Additives: Preservatives, Colour Additives, Flavour Enhancers, Emulsifiers.

Noodles: Rice, Vermicelli.

Sauces: Fish Sauce (Thipres), Hot Bean, Hoisin, Kikkoman Soya, Light Soya, L&P, Oyster, Prune Sauce, Stir Fry, Sweet Black Soya, Sweet Chilli, Tabasco, Mushroom Soya, Plum.

Sea Food (Canned): Prawn, Crab, Lobster, Shrimps, Oyster.

Mushrooms (Frozen): Straw, Abalone, White Coral, Morel.

Flour: Tapioca, Tempura, Dimsum, All Purpose (Kite), Gluten Potato (Holland).

Oriental Products: Penang Curry Paste, Massaman Curry Paste, Green Curry Paste (Thipres), Black Fungus, Coconut Cream, Coconut Milk.

Ahuja Vegetable Store

9am to 9pm

116, INA Market, New Delhi, Ph: 24644116, 24626129

Fruits: Strawberry, Sea Grape, American Apple, Queen Pineapple, Babacos, Blackberry, Blackcurrant, Blueberry, Carambola, Cranberry, Curuba, Dragon Fruit, Durian, Figs, Gooseberry, Grapefruit, Kaffir Lime, Kiwifruit, Longan, Mangosteen, Passion Fruit, Pomelo, Persimmon, Redcurrant, Raspberry, Rambutan, Thai Litchi, Peach, Tamarind, Plum, American Grapes, Japanese Melon, Chinese Apple.

Vegetables: Broccoli, Brussels Sprout, Chinese Broccoli, Oriental Mustard, Drumstick, Lolo Rosso & Frisse, Asparagus, Avocado, Celery, Artichoke, Cherry Tomato, Sweet Corn, Zucchini, Snow Pea, Peppers, Radicchio, Leeks, Fennel, Chinese Cabbage, Pok-Choi, Chicory.

Herbs: Basil, Chervil, Chives, Dill, Fennel, Lemongrass, Marjoram, Oregano, Mint, Parsley, Rosemary, Sage, Thyme.

Mushrooms: Button/White, Chestnut, Chanterelle, Oyster, Enoki, Shiitake, Matsutake, Truffle (White/Black), Morel, Paddy/Straw.

Agrim Sales

11am to 8pm

18, CSC 8, Sector 8, Rohini, Delhi, Ph:27944993, 27942164 Ph: 27944993

Oils: Argan, Avocado, Canola/Rapeseed, Flax Seed, Hemp Seed, Macadamia, Palm Kernel, Rice Bran, Safflower, Tea Oil, Walnut, Watermelon, Dill Seed, Rosemary, Tarragon, Thyme, Extra Virgin Olive, Virgin Olive, Pure Olive, Pomace Olive, Corn.

Food Additives: Preservatives, Colour Additives, Flavour Enhancers, Acidity Regulators.

Pastas: Spaghetti, Fusilli, Fettuccini, Lasagna, Penne, Bucatini, Cannelloni, Cappelletti, Macaroni, Mafalde, Vermicelli, Gnocchi, Linguine, Tubetti, Ravioli.

Noodles: Vermicelli, Udon, Glass, Spaghetti.

Sauces: Albert, Alfredo, Barbecue, Bercy, Brown, Chasseur, Choron, Crème Anglaise, Figaro, Hard Sauce, Harissa, Hoisin, Louis, Oyster, Plum, Romesco, Shrimp, Tabasco, Verte, Worcestershire.

Herbs: Angelica, Basil, Bay, Chervil, Chives, Dill, Fennel, Lemongrass, Marjoram, Oregano, Mint, Parsley, Rosemary, Sage, Tarragon, Thyme.

Sea Food (Frozen): Smoked Salmon, Fresh Salmon, Salami, Sardine, Pink Salmon, Parma Ham.

Mushrooms: Button, Chestnut, Oyster, Enokitaki, Shiitake, Matsutake, Morel.

Flour: Arrowroot, Buckwheat, Chickpea, Maize Meal, Semolina.

Ajit Farms

9:30am to 10pm

■ **34, Malviya Nagar, New Delhi, Ph: 26685426, 26682665, 65682665**

Meat Products: Ham, Pork, Bacon, Salami, Sausage, Lamb Rack.

Allied Fruits & Florists

8am to9 pm

■ **58 B, Khan Market, New Delhi, Ph: 24642509, 24619310, 41757003**

Oils: Argan, Avocado, Canola, Rapeseed, Flax Seed, Hemp Seed, Macadamia, Safflower, Dill Seed, Rosemary, Tarragon, Thyme, Extra Virgin Olive, Virgin Olive, Pure Olive, Pomace Olive.

Pastas: Spaghetti, Fusilli, Fettuccine, Lasagna, Penne, Bucatini, Cannelloni, Cappelletti, Macaroni, Mafalde, Vermicelli, Gnocchi, Linguine, Tubetti, Ravioli.

Noodles: Rice, Vermicelli, Fettuccine, Glass, Spaghetti, Phad-Thai.

Fruits: Strawberry, Sea Grape, American Mayapple, Queen Pineapple, Babacos, Blackberry, Blackcurrant, Blueberry, Carambola, Cranberry, Curumba, Dragon Fruit, Pithaya, Durian, Feijoas, Fig, Gooseberry, Grapefruit, Grenadilla, Kaffir Lime, Kiwifruit, Kumquat, Longan, Mangosteen, Passion Fruit, Pomelo, Persimmon, Redcurrant, Raspberry, Rambutan, Ugli Fruit, Thai Litchi, Peaches, Tamarind Plum.

Vegetables: Broccoli, Brussels Sprout, Drumstick, Lolo Rosso, Frisse, Asparagus, Avocado, Celery, Artichoke, Cherry Tomato, Sweet Corn, Zucchini, Snow Pea, Pepper, Radicchio, Leeks, Fennel, Chinese Cabbage, Pok-Choi, Chicory.

Sauces: Hollandaise (Emulsified Sauce), Alfredo, Barbecue, Bercy, Bigarade, Brown, Chasseur, Cocktail, Cranberry, Crème Anglaise, Figaro, Harissa, Hoisin, Oyster, Parisienne, Plum, Romesco, Shrimp, Tabasco, Verte, Worcestershire.

Syrups: Grain, Birch, Maple, Berry, Corn, Palm/Date, Golden, Black Treacle, Dark Syrup, Molasses, Fruit, Flower (Rose/Black/Locust).

Herbs: Angelica, Basil, Bay, Chervil, Chive, Dill, Fennel, Lemongrass, Marjoram, Oregano, Mint, Parsley,

Rosemary, Sage, Tarragon, Thyme.

Sea Food (Canned): Prawn, Lobster, Squid, Crab, Fish.

Cheese: Camembert, Cheddar, Colby, Wellington, Stilton, Feta, Gorgonzola, Emmental, Gouda, Edam, Gruye're, Havarti, Limburger, Mascarpone, Mozzarella, Parmesan, Romano Ricotta, Roquefort, Swiss.

Mushrooms: Button/White, Chestnut, Chanterelle, Oyster, Enoki, Shiitake, Matsutake, Morels, Paddy/Straw.

Miscellaneous Products: Olive, Salad Dressing.

Meat Products: Duck, Turkey, Cornfed Chicken, Pork, Bacon, Quail, Pancetta, Ham, Salami, Sausage, Frankfurter, Lamb Rack.

Amrit

10am to 7pm

Aashirwad Agencies, 58-59, Kalu Sarai, Sarvapriya Vihar, New Delhi, Ph: 41828234, 9811011053

Cheese: Camembert, Cheddar, Colby, Wellington, Stilton, Feta, Gorgonzola, Emmental, Gouda, Edam, Havarti, Romano, Ricotta, Roquefort, Swiss.

Oils: Argan, Avocado, Hemp Seed, Macadamia, Tea, Walnut, Dill Seed, Rosemary, Tarragon, Thyme, Extra Virgin Olive, Virgin Olive, Pure Olive, Pomace Olive.

Pastas: Spaghetti, Fusilli, Fettuccine, Lasagne, Penne, Bucatini, Cannelloni, Cappelletti, Macaroni, Mafalde, Vermicelli, Gnocchi, Linguine, Tubetti, Ravioli.

Noodles: Rice, Vermicelli, Fettuccine, Udon, Glass, Spaghetti, Phad-Thai.

Vegetables: Asparagus, Avocado, Celery, Artichoke, Cherry Tomato, Sweet Corn.

Sauces: Barbecue, Brown, Cocktail, Cranberry, Crème Anglaise, Figaro, Hoisin, Oyster, Parisienne, Piquante, Plum, Shrimp, Sofrito, Tabasco, Verte, Worcestershire.

Syrups: Grain, Birch, Maple, Berry, Corn, Palm/Date, Golden, Black Treacle, Dark Syrup, Molasses, Fruit, Cocktail and Mocktail, Flower (Rose/Black/Locust).

Herbs: Angelica, Basil, Chive, Dill, Fennel, Parsley, Rosemary, Sage.

Sea Food (Frozen): Lobster, Prawn, Scallop, Shrimp, Smoked Salmon.

Mushrooms: Button/White, Chestnut, Chanterelle, Cepes, Oyster, Enoki, Shiitake, Matsutake, Truffle (White/Black), Morel, Paddy/Straw.

Flour: Dim Sum, Tempura.

Miscellaneous Products: Bamboo Shoot, Bean Curd, Canned Jalapeno, Miso Paste, Bakery Items, Bar Items, Satay Paste.

Meat Products: Lamb Rack (New Zealand), Parma Ham.

Anand

AC

10am to 9pm

63 A, Khan Market, New Delhi, Ph: 24626517, 24641804, 9312444441

Oils: Argan, Avocado, Canola/Rapeseed, Flax Seed, Hemp Seed, Macadamia, Palm Kernel, Rice Bran, Walnut, Dill Seed, Rosemary, Tarragon, Thyme, Extra Virgin Olive, Virgin Olive, Pure Olive, Pomace Olive, Corn.

Food Additives: Preservatives, Colour Additives, Flavour Enhancers, Emulsifiers, Stabilisers, Thickeners, Binders, Texturisers, Firming Agents, Dough Strengtheners, Conditioners, Sweeteners, Acidity Regulators, Leavening Agents, Anti-Caking Agents, Humectants, Colour Fixatives.

Pastas: Spaghetti, Fusilli, Fettuccine, Lasagna, Penne, Bucatini, Cannelloni, Cappelletti, Macaroni, Mafalde, Vermicelli, Gnocchi, Linguine, Tubetti, Ravioli.

Noodles: Rice, Vermicelli, Fettuccine, Spaghetti.

Sauces: Barbecue, Bercy, Cocktail, Cranberry, Crème Anglaise, Harissa, Hoisin, Marinara, Newburg, Normande, Oyster, Plum, Romesco, Shrimp, Worcestershire.

Syrups: Grain, Birch, Maple, Berry, Corn, Palm/Date, Golden, Black Treacle, Fruit, Flower(Rose/Black/Locust).

Herbs: Angelica, Basil, Bay, Chervil, Chives, Dill, Fennel, Lemongrass, Marjoram, Oregano, Mint, Parsley, Rosemary, Sage, Tarragon, Thyme.

Sea Food (Canned): Prawn, Tiger Jumbo Prawn, King Prawn, Crab, Shrimp, Smoked Oyster, Tuna, Sardine, Mackerel, Kipper Fillet, Hering Fillet, Pink Salmon.

Cheese: Camembert, Cheddar, Colby, Wellington, Stilton, Feta, Gorgonzola, Emmental, Gouda, Edam, Gruye're, Havarti, Limburger, Mascarpone, Mozzarella, Parmesan, Romano, Ricotta, Roquefort, Swiss.

Mushrooms: Button/White, Chestnut, Chanterelle, Oyster, Shiitake.

Flour: Buckwheat, Semolina.

Meat Products (Canned): Duck, Turkey, Pork, Bacon, Quail, Salami, Sausage, Frankfurter.

Bahety Overseas

AC
9.30am to 7.30pm

B 135, Panchsheel Vihar, Khirki Malviya Nagar, New Delhi, Ph: 29541509, 29541742

Pastas: Spaghetti, Fusili, Fettuccini, Lasagne, Penne, Bucatini, Cannelloni, Cappelletti, Macaroni, Mafalde, Vermicelli, Gnocchi, Linguine, Tubetti, Ravioli.

Noodles: Rice, Fettuccine, Spaghetti.

Syrups: Grain, Birch, Maple Syrup, Berry, Corn, Palm/Date, Golden, Black Treacle, Dark Syrup, Molasses, Bar Syrup, Fruit, Fiesta Cocktail, Sparkling Juice, Cocktails, Cakes, Juices, Biscuits.

Bhutani

AC
9am to 11pm

A 26, NDSE II, New Delhi, Ph: 41644488, 9910120120

Oils: Canola/Rapeseed, Rice Bran, Safflower, Dill Seed, Rosemary, Tarragon, Thyme, Extra Virgin Olive, Pure Olive, Pomace Olive.

Food Additives: Preservatives, Colour Addictives, Flavour Enhancers, Emulsifiers, Stabilisers, Thickeners, Binders, Texturisers, Firming Agents, Dough Strengtheners, Conditioners, Sweeteners, Acidity Regulators, Leavening Agents, Anti-caking Agents,

Humectants, Colour Fixatives.

Pastas: Spaghetti, Fusilli, Fettuccine, Lasagne, Penne, Bucatini, Cannelloni, Cappelletti, Macaroni, Mafalde, Vermicelli, Ravioli.

Noodles: Rice, Vermicelli, Fettuccine, Spaghetti.

Sauces: Tabasco, Worcestershire.

Syrups: Birch, Maple, Corn, Fruit.

Sea Food (Canned): Prawn, Tiger Jumbo Prawn, Lobster, Red Snapper, Halibut, Pomfret, Shrimp, Pink Salmon.

Cheese: Camembert, Cheddar, Feta, Gorgonzola, Emmental, Gouda, Edam, Gruye're, Havarti, Limburger, Mascarpone, Mozzarella, Parmesan, Romano, Roquefort, Swiss.

Mushrooms: Button/White, Chestnut, Chanterelle, Oyster, Morel.

Miscellaneous Products: Olive, Salad Dressing, Canned Jalepeno.

Big Apple

AC SS

- **28/13, Street 14, Main 60 Feet Road, Vishwas Nagar, New Delhi, Ph: 22304032**
- **S 11, East of Kailash, New Delhi, Ph: 9313928422**
- **D 2/8, Ground Floor, Model Town, Delhi, Ph: 9313928430**
- **B3/24, Model Town I, Opp. Durga Mandir, Delhi, Ph: 32054961, 9313928414**
- **38, Vikas Marg, Ram Vihar, Delhi, Ph: 43011835, 9313928449**
- **B 5/9, Opposite Bhagat Singh Park, Yamuna Vihar, Delhi, Ph: 22916234, 9313928447**
- **80, Main Road, Vikas Marg, Defence Enclave, New Delhi, Ph: 22457559, 9313928451**
- **10, Opposite AGCR Enclave, Shanti Vihar, New Delhi, Ph: 43035092, 9313928456**
- **S 14, Janta Market, Rajouri Garden, Delhi, Ph: 45517304, 9313928410**
- **19-20, G Block, Community Centre, Vikas Puri, New Delhi, Ph: 45531076, 9313928409**
- **A 7, Shyam Nagar, New Delhi, Ph: 25987126, 9313928411**
- **14/472, Opposite Meera Bagh, Near St. Marks School, Sunder Vihar, New Delhi, Ph: 42334835, 9313928427**
- **412-413, Kakrola Housing Complex, Near Metro Pillar 792, Dwarka Mod, New Delhi, Ph: 25331510, 9313928453**
- **11/18, East Patel Nagar Market, New Delhi, Ph: 42482020, 9313928401**
- **Block A, DDA Commercial Complex, Naraina Vihar, New Delhi, Ph: 25778454, 9313928405**
- **82, Double Storey, New Rajinder Nagar, Delhi, Ph: 45086158, 9313928407**
- **2218, Paharganj, Delhi, Ph: 23586338, 9313928440**
- **ER 25, Inder Puri, New Delhi, Ph: 25833142, 9313928441**
- **5C/9, New Rohtak Road, Karol Bagh, Delhi, Ph: 9313928465**
- **E 22, Hauz Khas Market, New Delhi, Ph: 41656060, 9313928403**
- **L 1, Lajpat Nagar I, New Delhi, Ph: 9313928404**

■ 389, Block, Street 11, Old Rang Puri Road, Mahipal Pur, New Delhi, Ph: 26781831, 9313928432

■ A 134, New Friends Colony, Near Ashram Chowk, Taimoor Nagar, New Delhi, Ph: 26921288, 9313928442

■ A 268 Defence Colony, New Delhi, Ph: 46543959, 9313928443

■ 943, Nehru Road, Arjun Nagar, Kotla Mubarakpur, New Delhi, Ph: 24647674, 9313928454

■ JC 44, Malviya Nagar, Khirki Extension, New Delhi, Ph: 46036481, 9313928457

■ C 4, Freedom Fighter Colony, Neb Sarai, New Delhi, Ph: 29533683, 9313928460

■ K 103, Main Road, Kalkaji, New Delhi, Ph: 26228106

■ 7, CSC 9, DDA Market, Sector 16, Rohini, Delhi, Ph: 27298044, 9313928435

■ 5-6, Hudson Lane, Kingsway Camp, New Delhi, Ph: 47019324, 9313928419

■ 28-29, CSC 9, G Block, D.D.A Market, Sector 15, Rohini, Delhi, Ph: 27298124, 9313928420

■ 11, CSC 3, D 2 Block DDA Market, Sector 11, Rohini, Delhi, Ph: 27570538, 9313928421

■ 1-2, CSC 8, DDA Market, Opposite Remal Public School, Sector 3, Rohini, Delhi, Ph: 27514636, 9313928424

■ HP 9, Maurya Enclave, Pitampura, Opposite Gopal Mandir, New Delhi, Ph: 47562517, 9313928429

■ D 2/8, Model Town III, New Delhi, Ph: 47019427, 9313928430.

■ 10, DDA Market, Vaishali, Pitampura, Delhi, Ph: 47023915, 9313928439

■ 704, Opposite Batra Hall, Mukherji Nagar, Delhi, Ph: 27604810, 9313928445

■ AM 34, Shalimar Bagh, Delhi, Ph: 47037924, 9313928448

■ A 1/13, Near Laxmibai College, Shakti Nagar Extension, New Delhi

■ CSC 9, Shop 7, Sector 16, Opposite DDA Market, Ph: 9313928418

■ Shop No. 28, G Block, DDA Market, Sector 15, Rohini, Delhi, Ph: 9313928420

■ Shop No. 1/2, CSC 8, Ground & First Floor, Sector 3, Rohini, Delhi, Ph: 9313928424

■ Shop S23/11, CSC 3, Sector 11, Rohini, Delhi, Ph: 9313928421

■ Shop 87, Shyam Nagar, Khyal Road, New Delhi, Ph: 9313928421

Oils: Argan, Avocado, Canola/Rapeseed, Flax Seed, Hemp Seed, Macadamia, Palm Kernel, Rice Bran, Safflower, Tea Oil, Extra Virgin Olive, Virgin Olive, Pure Olive, Pomace Olive, Corn.

Food Additives: Preservatives, Colour Additives, Flavour Enhancers, Acidity Regulators.

Pastas: Spaghetti, Fusilli, Fettuccine, Cannelloni, Cappelletti, Macaroni, Vermicelli.

Fruits: Strawberry Tree, Sea Grape, American Mayapple, Queen Pineapple, Grapefruit, Kiwifruit, Thai Litchi, Peach, Tamarind, Plum.

Vegetables: Broccoli, Brussels Sprout, Chinese Broccoli, Oriental Mustard,

Malabar Gourd, Drumstick, Lolo Rosso, Frisse, Asparagus, Avocado, Celery, Cherry Tomato, Sweet Corn, Zucchini, Pepper, Leeks Fennel, Pok-Choi.

Sauces: Espagnole, Velouté, Béchamel, Vinaigrette, Albert, Alfredo, Allemande, Aurore, Barbecue, Bernaise ,

Bercy, Bigarade, Bordelaise, Brown, Chasseur, Choron, Cocktail, Colbert, Cranberry, Crème Anglaise, Diable, Figaro, Genevoise, Hard, Harissa, Hoisin, Louis, Lyonnaise, Maltaise, Marguery, Marinara, Melba, Mornay, Newburg, Normande, Oyster, Parisienne, Piquante, Plum, Puttanesca, Ranchero, Rémoulade, Romesco, Rouille, Shrimp, Sofrito, Tabasco, Verte, Worcestershire.

Syrups: Grain, Birch, Maple, Fruit, Flower (Rose/Black/Locust).

Herbs: Angelica, Basil, Bay, Chervil, Chives, Dill, Fennel, Lemongrass, Marjoram, Oregano, Mint, Parsley, Rosemary, Sage, Tarragon, Thyme, Artemesia, Kalmegh.

Sea Food (Frozen): Prawns, Fish.

Cheese: Cheddar, Colby, Gorgonzola, Emmental, Gouda, Edam, Mozzarella, Parmesam, Swiss.

Mushrooms: Button, Oyster.

Caspian Caviar & Fine Food

AC
10am to 6pm

B 33, Kailash Colony, New Delhi, Ph: 9811478506, 41631484

Caviar: Sevruga, Beluga, Osetra, Trout Roe, Salmon Roe.

Sea Food (Frozen): Blue Chip Salmon, Scottish Salmon, Salmon Roe.

Miscellaneous Products: Cornfed Chicken, Duck Breast, Goose Foie Gras, Duck Foie Gras, Duck Breast Magret, Processed Foie Gras, Italian Truffle, Smoked Kipper, Smoked Mackerel, Smoked Trout Fillet.

Ceegate Overseas

AC
9.30am to 6.30pm

H 3/1A, Krishna Nagar, Delhi, Ph: 9810231199, 9871444668

Sea Food (Frozen): Canadian Lobster, Salmon, Kings/Queen Scallop, Halibut.

Meat Products: Pork Bacon, Prostuitto(Canada), Pancetta, Lamb Rack.

Chicken Ette

10am to 9pm

39, LSC, New Friends Colony, New Delhi, Ph: 26847157, 26848746

Sea Food: Prawn, Tiger Jumbo Prawn, King Prawn, Lobster, Squid, Pomfret, Red Snapper, Crab Meat, Shrimp, Fish.

Meat Products: Duck, Turkey, Pork, Bacon, Ham, Salami, Sausage, Frankfurter, Lamb Rack.

Chicken Ette

AC
10am to 9pm

11-12, Sector 15, Faridabad, Ph: 95129-2290191, 2284210

Sauces: Albert, Alfredo, Barbecue, Bercy, Brown, Chasseur, Choron, Crème Anglaise, Figaro, Hard Sauce, Harissa, Hoisin, Louis, Oyster, Plum, Romesco, Shrimp, Tabasco, Verte, Worcestershire and White Sauce.

Syrups: Grain, Birch, Maple, Flower, Corn, Palm/Date, Golden, Black Treacle, Dark Syrup, Molasses.

Sea Food: Prawn, Tiger Jumbo Prawn, King Prawn, Lobsters, Squid, Pomfret, Red Snapper, Crab Meat, Shrimp, Fish.

Meat Products: Duck, Turkey, Pork, Bacon, Ham, Salami, Sausage, Frankfurter, Lamb Rack.

Dairy Craft India

AC
9:30am to 7:30pm

32, Main Market, Hudson Lane, Kingsway Camp, Model Town, GTB Nagar, Delhi, Ph: 27232539

Oils: Extra Virgin Olive, Virgin Olive, Pure Olive, Pomace Olive, Corn.

Pastas: Fusilli, Lasagne, Penne, Bucatini, Cannelloni, Cappelletti, Macaroni, Mafalde, Vermicelli, Gnocchi, Linguine, Tubetti, Ravioli.

Cheese: Cheddar, Feta, Gorgonzola, Emmental, Gouda and Edam, Gruyere, Havarti, Mascarpone, Mozzarella, Parmesan, Ricotta, Swiss, Roquefort.

Meat Products: Turkey, Bacon, Ham, Salami.

Debon Meat Shop

10am to 9pm

D 1, Alaknanda Shopping Complex, Sector 28, Noida, Ph: 95120-2452999

Sea Food: Prawn, Squid, Red Snapper, Shrimp, Sardines, Salmon, Tiger Prawn.

Meat Products: Ham, Sausage, Salami, Frankfurter, Bacon, Lamb Rack, Duck.

Dee's Chawla Store

AC
9am to 10pm

6, Central Market, Pocket A, Mayur Vihar Phase II, Delhi, Ph: 22772796, 9810312013

Oils: Argan, Hemp Seed, Macadamia, Palm Kernel, Dill Seed, Rosemary, Tarragon, Thyme, Extra Virgin Olive, Virgin Olive, Pure Olive, Pomace Olive.

Food Additives: Preservatives, Colour Additives, Flavour Enhancers, Stabilisers, Thickeners, Dough Strengtheners, Conditioners, Sweeteners.

Pastas: Spaghetti, Fusilli, Fettuccine, Lasagne, Penne, Bucatini, Cannelloni, Cappelletti, Macaroni, Mafalde, Vermicelli, Gnocchi, Linguine, Tubetti, Ravioli.

Noodles: Vermicelli, Fettuccine, Spaghetti.

Fruits (Canned): Pear, Peach, Red Cherry, Fruit Cocktail, Pineapple Slice, Corn.

Vegetables (Canned): Asparagus, Baby Corn.

Sauces: Barbecue, Brown, Cocktail, Figaro, Hoisin, Oyster, Romesco, Shrims, Verte, Worcestershire.

Syrups: Grain, Birch, Maple,

Flower (Rose/Black/ Locust), Berry, Corn, Palm/Date, Golden, Fruit.

Herbs: Angelica, Basil, Bay, Chervil, Chives, Dill, Fennel, Lemongrass, Marjoram, Oregano, Mint, Parsley, Rosemary, Sage, Tarragon, Thyme.

Sea Food (Frozen): Prawn, Tiger Jumbo Prawn, King Prawn, Lobster, Squid, Pomfret, Red Snapper, Crab, Fish.

Cheese: Camembert, Cheddar, Feta, Gouda, Edam, Mascarpone, Mozzarella, Parmesan, Romano, Ricotta, Roquefort, Swiss.

Mushrooms: Button/White, Oyster.

Flour: Arrowroot, Buckwheat, Chickpea, Maize Meal, Semolina.

Defence Store

AC 8am to 10pm

38, Defence Colony Market, New Delhi, Ph: 41551305, 24333152, 24333693

Oils: Argan, Canola/Rape Seed, Rice Bran, Sesame, Extra Virgin Olive, Virgin Olive, Pure Olive, Pomace Olive, Corn.

Food Additives: Preservatives, Colour Additives, Flavour Enhancers, Emulsifiers, Stabilisers, Thickeners, Binders, Texturisers, Firming Agents, Dough Strengtheners, Conditioners, Sweeteners, Acidity Regulators, Leavening Agents, Anti-Caking Agents, Humectants, Thickeners, Colour Fixatives.

Pastas: Spaghetti, Fusilli, Fettuccine, Lasagne, Penne, Bucatini, Cannelloni, Cappelletti, Macaroni, Mafalde, Vermicelli, Ravioli.

Noodles: Rice, Vermicelli, Fettuccine, Glass, Spaghetti, Phad-Thai.

Sauces: Cranberry, Hoisin, Oyster, Plum, Tabasco, Pesto, Worcestershire.

Syrups: Maple, Golden.

Herbs: Angelica, Basil, Bay, Chervil, Chives, Dill, Fennel, Lemongrass, Marjoram, Oregano, Mint, Parsley, Rosemary, Sage, Tarragon, Thyme.

Sea Food (Frozen): Prawn, Tiger Jumbo Prawn, King Prawn, Lobster, Pomfret, Red Snapper, Crab, Shrimp, Octopus, Oyster.

Cheese: Camembert, Cheddar, Stilton, Feta, Emmental, Gouda, Edam, Gruyere, Havarti, Mascarpone, Mozzarella, Parmesan, Ricotta, Roquefort.

Mushrooms (Canned): Button/White, Chestnut, Chanterelle, Oyster, Enokitake, Shiitake, Matsutake, Morel, Paddy/Straw, Truffle.

Flour: Maize Meal, Semolina.

Miscellaneous Products: Olives, Coconut Milk, Gherkins.

Meat Products (Canned): Duck, Turkey, Cornfed Chicken, Pork, Bacon, Quail, Pancetta, Ham, Salami, Sausage, Frankfurter, Lamb Rack.

Dera Farms

AC 9am to 9pm

D 429, Defence Colony, New Delhi, Ph: 24643491, 9312479551, 9810271540

Pastas: Spaghetti, Fusilli, Fettuccine, Lasagne, Penne, Bucatini, Cannelloni, Cappelletti, Macaroni, Mafalde, Vermicelli, Gnocchi, Linguine, Tubetti, Ravioli.

Noodles: Rice, Vermicelli, Fettuccine, Udon, Glass, Spaghetti.

Vegetable (Organic): Broccoli, Brussels Sprout, Drumstick, Asparagus, Celery, Artichoke, Lettuce, Celery, Cherry Tomato, Sweet Corn, Pepper, Leek, Fennel, Chinese Cabbage, Pok-Choi.

Sauces: Barbecue, Bernaise, Bercy, Bigarade, Bordelaise, Brown, Chasseur, Choron, Cocktail, Colbert, Cranberry, Oyster, Parisienne, Piquante, Plum, Puttanesca, Ranchero, Rémoulade, Romesco, Rouille, Shrimp, Sofrito, Tabasco, Verte, Worcestershire, White, Teriyaki, Hoisin, Tartare.

Syrups: Birch, Maple, Berry, Corn, Fruits.

Herbs: Angelica, Basil, Bay, Chervil, Chives, Dill, Fennel, Lemongrass, Marjoram, Oregano, Mint, Parsley, Rosemary, Sage, Tarragon, Thyme.

Cheese: Camembert, Cheddar, Feta, Gouda, Edam, Mozarella, Parmesan.

Mushrooms: Button, Oyster.

Meat Products: Chicken, Fish, Seekh Kebab, Sausage, Frankfurter, Ham Salami.

Ever Green Veg & Fruit

8am to 9pm

176, INA Market, New Delhi, Ph: 24635753, 24646663, 9811339376

Fruits: Strawberry, Sea Grape, American Apple, Queen Pineapple, Babacos, Blackberry, Blackcurrant, Blueberry, Carambola, Cranberry, Feijaos, Figs, Gooseberry, American Mayapple, Grenadilla, Kafirlime, Kumquat, Longan, Mangosteen, Passion Fruit, Pomelo, Persimmon, Redcurrant, Raspbeeries, Rambutan, Ugli Fruit, Thai Litchi, Peach, Tamarind, Plum, Kiwifruit, Longan, Mangosteen, Pomelo, Persimmon, Redcurrant, Raspberries, Rambutan, Thai Litchi, Peaches, Tamarind, Plum, American Grapes, Japanese Melon, Chinese Apple.

Vegetables: Broccoli, Brussels Sprout, Chinese Broccoli, Oriental Mustard, Malabar Gourd, Drumstick, Lolo Rosso, Frisse, Asparagus, Avocado, Celery, Artichoke, Cherry Tomato, Sweet Corn, Zucchini, Snow Pea, Pepper, Radicchio, Leeks, Fennel, Chinese Cabbage, Pok-Choi, Chicory, Chives, Parsley, Pipanto, Lettuce, Kaffir Leaf, Basil Leaf, Thai Ginger.

Mushrooms: Button/White, Chestnut, Chanterelle, Oyster, Enokitake , Shiitake, Matsutake, Morel, Paddy/Straw, Truffle.

Miscellaneous Products: Bamboo Shoots.

Exotique Concepts

AC
10am to 6pm

C 24, Sector 6, Noida, Ph: 95120-4350090

Miscellaneous Products: (Spices) All spices which are used in Indian Cuisine like Qorma Masala, Achar Ghost Masala, Biryani Masala, Haleem Masala.

First Bite Fruit & Vegetable

AC

10am to 10pm

A 309, Azadpur Veg Market, Delhi, Ph: 9899458294, 9810513709

Fruits: Strawberry, Sea Grape, American Mayapple, Queen Pineapple, Babacos, Blackberry, Blackcurrant, Blueberry, Carambola, Cranberry, Curuba, Dragon Fruit, Pithaya, Durian, Feijoas, Fig, Gooseberry, Grapefruit, Grenadilla, Kaffir Lime, Pears, Kiwifruit, Kumquat, Longan, Mangosteen, Passion Fruit, Pomelo, Persimmon, Redcurrant, Raspberry, Rambutan, Ugli Fruit, Thai Litchi, Peach, Tamarind, Plum.

Vegetables: Broccoli, Brussels Sprout, Chinese Broccoli, Oriental Mustard, Malabar Gourd, Drumstick, Lettuce, Spring Onion, Red Cabbage, Chives, Dill, Lolo Rosso, Frisse, Asparagus, Avocado, Celery, Artichoke, Cherry Tomato, Sweet Corn, Zucchini, Snow Pea, Pepper, Radicchio, Leek, Fennel, Chinese Cabbage, Pok-Choi, Chicory, Parsley.

Flanders Dairy

AC

10am to 5pm

C 23, South Extension Part II, New Delhi, Ph: 26253789, 41640438

H 3, Qutab Plaza, Phase II, Gurgaon, Ph: 95124-26357599

Cheese: Bocconcini, Gouda (Black Pepper Gouda, Cumin Gouda, Smoked Gouda), Italian Mozzarella, Kwark, Mascarpone, Ricotta, Scamorza, Sour Cream, Unsalted Butter.

Food Max

10am to 7pm

252, Shahpur Jat, Upper Ground Floor, Near Panchsheel Community Centre, New Delhi, Ph: 41730226-7, 9212010101

Oils: Extra Virgin Olive, Virgin Olive, Pure Olive, Pomace Olive, Olive Classico, Sesame.

Pastas: Spaghetti, Fusilli, Fettuccine, Lasagne, Penne, Bucatini, Cannelloni, Cappelletti, Macaroni, Mafalde, Vermicelli, Gnocchi, Linguine, Tubetti, Ravioli.

Noodles: Rice, Vermicelli, Fettuccine.

Sauces: Alfredo, Barbecue, Black Bean, Hot Szchewan, Thai Chilli, Mushroom Veg Oyster, Salsa, Hoisin, Plum, Shrimp, Tabasco, Worstershire, White.

Syrups: Margarita Mix, Blue Curacao, Grenadine, Bloody Mary, Hazelnut, Coconut, Blackcurrant, Cinnamon, Caramel.

Herbs: Angelica, Basil, Bay, Chervil, Chives, Dill, Fennel, Lemongrass, Marjoram, Oregano, Mint, Parsley, Rosemary, Sage, Tarragon, Thyme, Sumak Powder, Zataar Powder.

Sea Food (Canned): Kippler, Fillet, Wild Salmon, Tuna Chunks, Sardines in Olive Oil.

Cheese: Camembert, Cheddar, Colby, Wellington, Stilton, Feta, Gorgonzola, Emmental, Gouda, Edam, Gruyere, Havarti, Limburger, Mascarpone, Mozzarella, Parmesan, Romano, Bay Gouda, Boursin, Ricotta, Roquefort, Swiss.

French Farms

AC 8am to 5pm

■ Bilaspur, Only Door Delivery, Ph: 9810166196, 9810314186.

Vegetables (Organic): Lettuce, Baby Carrot, Broccoli, Chinese Broccoli, Red Raddish, Fennel, Baby Turnip.

Herbs: Basil, Tarragon, Oregano, Garlic Chives, Parsley, Dill, Marjoram, Sage.

Meat Products: Chicken, Free Range Chicken, Japanese Quail, Guinea, Fowl, Turkey, Muscovy Duck, Pork.

Garg Dastak

AC 11am to 10pm

■ LG 44/45, DT Mega Mall, DLF City Phase I, Gurgaon, Ph: 95124-4380008

Oils: Extra Virgin Olive, Virgin Olive, Pure Olive, Pomace Olive.

Food Additives: Preservatives, Colour Additives, Flavour Enhancers, Sweeteners, Acidity Regulators, Thickeners, Colour Fixatives.

Pastas: Spaghetti, Fusilli, Fettuccine, Lasagna, Penne, Bucatini, Cannelloni, Cappelletti, Macaroni, Mafalde, Vermicelli, Gnocchi, Linguine, Tubetti, Ravioli.

Noodles: Rice, Vermicelli, Fettuccine, Udon, Glass, Spaghetti.

Sauces: Barbecue, Brown, Cranberry, Crème Anglaise, Harissa, Hoisin, Oyster, Plum, Tabasco, Verte, Worcestershire, White.

Syrups: Grain, Birch, Maple, Flower (Rose/Black/ Locust), Berry, Corn, Fruit.

Herbs: Angelica, Basil, Bay, Chervil, Chives, Dill, Fennel, Lemongrass, Marjoram, Oregano, Mint, Parsley, Rosemary, Sage, Tarragon, Thyme.

Cheese: Cheddar, Gorgonzola, Mozzarella.

Gogia's

AC SS 10am to 9pm

■ 280, INA Market, New Delhi, Ph: 24624809, 24624929, 24629944, 24644618

Oils: Argan, Avocado, Canola/Rapeseed, Macadamia, Thyme, Extra Virgin Olive, Virgin Olive, Pure Olive, Pomace Olive, Corn.

Food Additives: Preservatives, Colour Additives, Flavour Enhancers, Sweeteners.

Pastas: Spaghetti, Fusilli, Fettuccine, Lasagne, Penne, Bucatini, Cannelloni, Cappelletti, Macaroni, Mafalde, Vermicelli, Gnocchi, Linguine, Tubetti, Ravioli

Noodles: Rice, Vermicelli, Fettuccine, Phad-Thai.

Fruits: Strawberry Tree, Sea Grape, American Mayapple, Queen Pineapple, Babacos, Blackberry, Blackcurrant, Blueberry, Carambola, Cranberry, Curuba, Dragon Fruit, Pithaya, Durian, Feijoas, Figs, Gooseberry, Grapefruit, Grenadilla, Kaffir Lime, Kiwifruit, Kumquat, Longan, Mangosteen, Passion Fruit, Pomelo, Persimmon, Redcurrant, Raspberry, Rambutan, Ugli Fruit, Thai Litchi, Peach, Tamarind, Plum.

Sauces: Barbecue, Hoisin, Marinara, Melba, Oyster, Parisienne, Piquante, Plum,

Sofrito, Tabasco, Verte, Worcestershire, White Sauces.

Syrups: Grain, Birch, Maple, Flower (Rose/Black/ Locust), Berry, Corn, Palm/Date, Golden, Black Treacle, Dark, Molasses, Fruit.

Herbs: Angelica, Basil, Bay, Chervil, Chives, Dill, Fennel, Lemongrass, Marjoram, Oregano, Mint, Parsley, Rosemary, Sage, Tarragon, Thyme.

Cheese: Camembert, Cheddar, Colby, Wellington, Stilton, Feta, Gorgonzola, Emmental, Gouda, Edam, Gruyere, Havarti, Limburger, Mascarpone, Mozzarella, Parmesan, Romano, Ricotta, Roquefort, Swiss.

Mushrooms: Button/White, Oyster, Shiitake, Truffle (White/Black), Morel, Paddy/Straw.

Miscellaneous Products: Salad Dressing, Thai Sauce.

Meat Products (Canned): Sausage, Ham.

Green Chic Chop

AC, Card — 9.30am to 9.30pm

- **10 & 11, Shopping Centre, Pocket D, Alaknanda, New Delhi, Ph: 26039999**
- **1/2, Arjun Nagar, Safdarjung Enclave, New Delhi, Ph: 26108245**
- **4, CSCB 10 Market, Vasant Kunj, New Delhi, Ph: 26132222**

Meat Products: Bacon, Pork, Quail, Ham, Salami, Sausage, Frankfurter.

Green Vegetable Mart

Home delivery — 5am to 5pm

- **51, New Okhla Mandi, New Delhi, Ph: 9810771261**

Fruits: Strawberry Tree, Sea Grape, American Mayapple, Queen Pineapple, Babacos, Blackberry, Blackcurrant, Blueberry, Carambola, Cranberry, Curuba, Dragon Fruit, Pithaya, Durian, Feijoas, Fig, Gooseberry, Grapefruit, Grenadilla, Kaffir Lime, Kiwifruit, Kumquat, Longan, Mangosteen, Passion Fruit, Pomelo, Persimmon, Redcurrant, Raspberry, Rambutan, Ugli Fruit, Thai Litchi, Peach, Tamarind, Chokeberry, Plum.

Vegetables: Broccoli, Brussels Sprout, Chinese Broccoli, Oriental Mustard, Malabar Gourd, Drumstick, Carrot Baby, Beancurd, Dillleaf, Lettuce, Lolo Rosso, Frisse, Asparagus, Avocado, Celery, Artichoke, Cherry Tomato, Sweet Corn, Zucchini, Snow Pea, Pepper, Radicchio, Leek, Fennel, Chinese Cabbage, Pok-Choi, Chicory, Baby Corn, Chives.

Harmilapi

AC, Card, Home delivery — 10am to 10pm

- **13, Main Market, Malviya Nagar, New Delhi, Ph: 41831677, 9811655648**
- **No. 27, Opp. Swagat Hotel, Main Market, Malviya Nagar, New Delhi, 26672277, 26671481**

Oils: Argan, Avocado, Canola/Rapeseed, Flax Seed, Hemp Seed, Macadamia, Palm Kernel, Rice Bran, Tea Oil, Limes, Walnut, Watermelon, Dill Seed, Rosemary, Tarragon, Thyme, Extra Virgin Olive, Virgin

Olive, Pure Olive, Pomace, Corn.

Food Additives: Preservatives, Colour Additives, Flavour Enhancers, Emulsifiers, Stabilisers, Binders, Texturisers, Firming Agents, Dough Strengtheners, Conditioners, Sweeteners, Acidity Regulators, Leavening Agents, Anti-Caking Agents, Humectants, Thickeners, Colour Fixatives.

Pastas: Spaghetti, Fusilli, Fettuccine, Lasagne, Penne, Bucatini, Cannelloni, Cappelletti, Macaroni, Mafalde, Vermicelli, Gnocchi, Linguine, Tubetti, Ravioli.

Noodles: Rice, Vermicelli, Fettuccine.

Sauces: Espagnole, Velouté, Béchamel, Hollandaise, Vinaigrette, Albert, Alfredo, Allemande, Aurore, Barbecue, Bernaise, Bercy, Bigarade, Bordelaise, Brown, Chasseur, Choron, Cocktail, Colbert, Cranberry, Crème Anglaise, Diable, Figaro, Genevoise, Hard, Harissa, Hoisin, Louis, Lyonnaise, Maltaise, Marguery, Marinara, Melba, Mornay, Newburg, Normande, Oyster, Parisienne, Piquante, Plum, Puttanesca, Ranchero, Rémoulade, Romesco, Rouille, Shrimp, Sofrito, Tabasco, Verte, Worcestershire, White.

Syrups: Grain, Birch, Maple, Flower (Rose/Black/ Locust), Berry, Corn, Palm/Date, Golden, Black Treacle, Dark, Molasses, Fruit.

Herbs: Angelica, Basil, Bay, Chervil, Chives, Dill, Fennel, Lemongrass, Marjoram, Oregano, Mint, Parsley, Rosemary, Sage, Tarragon, Thyme.

Sea Food: Prawn, Halibut, Pomfret, Crab, Sardine, Pink Salmon, River Sole, Foie Gras.

Cheese: Camembert, Cheddar, Colby, Wellington, Stilton, Feta, Gorgonzola, Emmental, Gouda, Edam, Gruye're, Havarti, Limburger, Mascarpone, Mozzarella, Parmesan, Romano, Ricotta, Roquefort, Swiss.

Mushrooms: Button/White, Chestnut, Chanterelle, Oyster, Enokitake, Shiitake, Matsutake, Morel, Paddy/Straw, Truffle.

Miscellaneous Products: Dried Fresh Fruits (Papaya, Apricot, Mango, Pineapple, Guava), Olives, Fizz Water (Natural Sparkling Water), Australian Water, Flavoured Yoghurt (Blueberry), Canned Jalapeno, Truffles, Spanish Iranian Saffron.

Meat Products: Meat, Mortadella, Parma Ham, Pancetta, Speck, Chicken Sausage, Smoked Scarmoza, Chorizo, Smoked Bacon.

Holy Land

AC

10am to 6pm

D 154, New Rajendra Nagar, New Delhi, Ph: 65467167, 65464802

Pastas: 'Monte Regale' Italian Pasta.

Noodles: Rice, Fettuccine, Spaghetti, Phad-Thai.

Fruits: Red Cheery, Strawberry Tree, Sea Grape, American Mayapple, Queen Pineapple, Babacos, Blackberry, Blackcurrant, Blueberry, Carambola, Cranberry, Curuba, Dragon Fruit, Pithaya, Durian, Feijoas, Fig, Gooseberry, Grapefruit, Grenadilla, Kaffir Lime, Kiwifruit, Kumquat, Longan, Mangosteen, Passion Fruit, Pomelo, Persimmon, Redcurrant, Raspberry, Rambutan, Ugli Fruit, Thai Litchi, Peach, Tamarind, Plum.

Sauces: Thai Sweet Chilli, Worcestershire, Mustard, Mayonise.

Syrups: Grain, Birch, Maple Syrup, Flower, Berry, Corn, Golden, Black Treacle, Dark, Molasses, Fruit.

Herbs: Angelica, Basil, Bay, Chervil, Chives, Dill, Fennel, Lemongrass, Marjoram, Oregano, Mint, Parsley, Rosemary, Sage, Tarragon, Thyme.

Sea Food: Prawn, Tiger Jumbo Prawn, Scallop, Lobster, Squid, Mackerel, Red Snapper, Halibut, Pomfret, Crab.

Mushrooms: Button, Mushroom Slice.

Flour: Arrowroot, Buckwheat, Chickpea, Maize Meal, Semolina.

Miscellaneous Products: Fruit Cocktail, Pineapple Slice, Coconut Milk.

Meat Products: Mortadella, Parma Ham, Pancetta, Pure Pork, White Penkin, Chicken Sausage, Chicken Frankfurter, Provolone Fetta Grill, Smoked Scarmoza, Cured Chorizo, Smoked Bacon.

IFB Agro

9am to 7pm

Marine Division, A 56, Okhla Industrial Area, Phase 1, New Delhi, Ph: 9311441616, 9350739994

Herbs: Angelica, Basil, Bay, Chervil, Chives, Dill, Fennel, Lemongrass, Marjoram, Oregano, Mint, Parsley, Rosemary, Sage, Tarragon, Thyme.

Sea Food: Prawn, Tiger Jumbo Prawn, King Prawn, Lobster, Squid, Pomfret, Crab, Kettle Fish, Bekti Fillet, River Sole.

IFM Impex Global

AC SS
9.30am to 6pm

C 351/9, Majlis Park, Delhi, Ph: 27674010, 27670436

Sea Food: Prawn, Tiger Jumbo Prawn, King Prawn, Lobster, Squid, Pomfret, Red Snapper, Crab Meat, Shrimp, Fish.

Inder

SS
9am to 9pm

40, INA Market, New Delhi, Ph: 24694008, 24636623, 24619372, 9811166516

Oils: Extra Virgin Olive, Virgin Olive, Pure Olive, Pomace Olive.

Pastas: Spaghetti, Fusilli, Fettuccine, Lasagne, Penne, Bucatini, Cannelloni, Cappelletti, Macaroni, Mafalde, Vermicelli, Gnocchi, Linguine.

Syrups: Maple, Berry, Corn, Golden, Black Treacle, Dark, Molasses, Fruit.

Herbs: Angelica, Basil, Bay, Chervil, Chives, Dill, Fennel, Lemongrass, Marjoram, Oregano, Mint, Parsley, Rosemary, Sage, Tarragon, Thyme.

Cheese: Camembert, Cheddar, Feta, Gorgonzola, Emmental, Gouda, Edam, Gruye're, Havarti, Mozzarella, Parmesan, Romano, Ricotta, Roquefort, Swiss.

Meat Products: Duck, Turkey, Cornfed Chicken, Pork, Bacon, Quail, Pancetta, Ham, Salami, Sausage, Frankfurter, Lamb Rack.

Indian Dairy

AC, Card, Home delivery
10am to 5pm

■ **WZ 598/C, Opposite Ram Mandir, Shree Nagar Enclave, Ranibagh, New Delhi, Ph: 27103229, 27182857, 9350186686**

Oils: Argan, Avocado, Palm Kernel, Rice Bran, Safflower, Tea Oil, Lime, Walnut, Watermelon, Dill Seed, Rosemary, Tarragon, Extra Virgin Olive, Virgin Olive, Pure Olive, Pomace Olive, Corn.

Cheese: Cheddar, Feta, Gouda, Edam, Wellington, Stilton Mascarpone, Mozzarella.

Jainsons

Home delivery
10am to 9pm

■ **278, INA Market, New Delhi, Ph: 24602250, 24653827, 9810268061**

Oils: Canola/Rapeseed, Macadamia, Safflower, Tea Oil, Dill Seed, Thyme, Extra Virgin Olive, Virgin Olive, Pure Olive, Pomace Olive, Corn.

Food Additives: Preservatives, Colour Additives, Flavour Enhancers, Sweeteners, Anti-Caking Agents.

Pastas: Spaghetti, Fusilli, Fettuccine, Lasagne, Penne, Bucatini, Cannelloni, Cappelletti, Macaroni, Mafalde, Vermicelli, Gnocchi, Linguine.

Noodles: Rice, Vermicelli, Fettuccine, Glass, Phad-Thai.

Fruits: Strawberry Tree, Sea Grape, American Mayapple, Queen Pineapple, Babacos, Blackberry, Blackcurrant, Blueberry, Carambola, Cranberry, Curuba, Dragon Fruit, Durian, Feijoas, Fig, Gooseberry, Grapefruit, Grenadilla, Kaffir Lime, Kiwifruit, Kumquat, Longan, Mangosteen, Passion Fruit, Pomelo, Persimmon, Redcurrant, Raspberries, Rambutan, Ugli Fruit, Thai Litchi, Peach, Tamarind, Plum.

Sauces: Barbecue, Colbert, Cranberry, Hoisin, Oyster, Plum, Tabasco, Abalone, Blackbean, Teriyaki.

Syrups: Grain, Birch, Maple, Flower (Rose/Black/ Locust), Berry, Corn, Palm/Date, Golden, Black Treacle, Dark, Molasses, Fruit.

Herbs: Angelica, Basil, Bay, Chervil, Chives, Dill, Fennel, Lemongrass, Marjoram, Oregano, Mint, Parsley, Rosemary, Sage, Tarragon, Thyme.

Sea Food: Prawn, Tiger Jumbo Prawn, King Prawn, Lobster, Squid, Pomfret, Crab, Kettle Fish, Bekti Fillet, River Sole.

Cheese: Camembert, Cheddar, Feta, Gorgonzola, Emmental, Gouda, Edam, Gruye're, Havarti, Limburger, Mascarpone, Mozzarella, Parmesan, Romano, Ricotta, Roquefort, Swiss.

Mushrooms: Button/White, Chestnut, Chanterelle, Oyster, Enokitake, Shiitake, Truffle (White/Black), Morels, Paddy/Straw.

Flour: Arrowroot, Buckwheat, Maize Meal, Semolina.

Miscellaneous Products: Salad Dressings, Vinegar.

Meat Products: Duck, Turkey, Cornfed Chicken, Pork, Bacon, Quail, Pancetta, Ham, Salami, Sausage, Frankfurter, Lamb Rack.

Khub Chand

AC 10am to 10pm

- K 20, Connaught Place, New Delhi, Ph: 23417515, 23412229
- 7, DDA Market, Yusuf Sarai, New Delhi, Ph: 26512279, 46056848

Meat Products: Pork without Skin, Chop, Fillet, Spare Rib, Sausage, Fresh Bacon Slice, Fresh Smoked Pork, Chicken Frankfurter, Smoked Chicken, Pork Salami, Pork Frankfurter, Pork Smoked Sausage, Pork Seekh Kabab, Chicken Ham, Chicken Salami.

KLG Imports and Exports

AC 7am to 8pm

- B 160, Near Fruit Market, Azadpur, New Delhi, Ph: 9311231001

Fruits: Strawberry Tree, Sea Grape, American Mayapple, Queen Pineapple, Babacos, Blackberry, Blackcurrant, Blueberry, Carambola, Cranberry, Curuba, Dragon Fruit, Pithaya, Durian, Feijoas, Fig, Gooseberry, Grapefruit, Grenadilla, Kaffir Lime, Kiwifruit, Kumquat, Longan, Mangosteen, Passion Fruit, Pomelo, Persimmon, Redcurrant, Raspberry, Rambutan, Ugli Fruit, Thai Litchi, Peach, Tamarind, Plum.

Kohinoor Food

AC 10am to 6pm

- 201, Vipps Center, Masjid Moth, Greater Kailash II, New Delhi, Ph: 41396810

Vegetables (Individually Quick Frozen): Broccoli, Brussels Sprout, Chinese Broccoli, Oriental Mustard, Malabar Gourd, Drumstick, Lolo Rosso, Asparagus, Avocado, Celery, Artichoke, Cherry Tomato, Sweet Corn, Zucchini, Snow Pea, Pepper, Radicchio, Leek, Fennel, Chinese Cabbage, Pok-Choi, Chicory, all Indian Vegetables.

Miscellaneous Products: Cooking Sauces, Cooking Pastes (Ginger, Chilli, Onion, Garlic).

Lakshmi

AC 8am to 9.30pm

- M 34, Greater Kailash Market I, New Delhi, Ph: 29221761, 29211462, 29211362

Oils: Canola/Rapeseed, Hemp Seed, Tea Oil, Thyme, Extra Virgin Olive, Virgin Olive, Pure Olive, Pomace Olive, Corn.

Food Additives: Preservatives, Sweeteners.

Pastas: Spaghetti, Fusilli, Fettuccine, Lasagna, Penne, Bucatini, Cannelloni, Cappelletti, Macaroni, Mafalde, Vermicelli, Gnocchi, Linguine, Tubetti, Ravioli.

Noodles: Rice, Vermicelli, Fettuccine, Spaghetti.

Sauces: Béchamel, Vinaigrette, Allemande, Barbecue, Bercy, Cocktail, Diable, Hoisin, Marguery, Marinara, Melba, Oyster, Plum, Puttanesca, Ranchero, Rémoulade, Romesco, Tabasco, Verte, Worcestershire, White.

Syrups: Grain, Birch, Maple, Berry, Corn, Palm/date, Golden, Dark, Molasses, Fruit.

Herbs: Angelica, Basil, Bay, Chervil, Chives, Dill, Fennel, Lemongrass, Marjoram, Oregano, Mint, Parsley, Rosemary, Sage, Tarragon, Thyme.

Sea Food: Prawn, Tiger Jumbo Prawn, Scallop, Lobster, Squid, Mackerel, Red Snapper, Halibut, Pomfret, Crab, Shrim, Octopus, Oyster, Sardine, Pink Salmon, River Sole, Foie Gras.

Cheese: Cheddar, Stilton, Gorgonzola, Gouda, Edam, Havarti, Limburger, Mozzarella, Parmesan, Romano, Ricotta, Roquefort, Swiss.

Mushrooms: Button, Oyster.

Flour: Chickpea, Semolina.

Meat Products (Tinned): Fish, Hams, Sausage.

Le Marche

9am to 9pm

- **58, Basant Lok, Vasant Vihar, New Delhi, Ph: 43232123, 9910386710, 9910386703**
- **58, Khan Market, New Delhi, Ph: 24640741**
- **4053, Select Citywalk, Saket, New Delhi, Ph: 40534555**
- **161 DLF, Saket, New Delhi, Ph: 9910602222, 9971735555**

Oils: Argan, Avocado, Canola/Rapeseed, Flax Seed, Hemp Seed, Macadamia, Palm Kernel, Rice Bran, Safflower, Tea Oil, Lime, Walnut, Watermelon, Dill Seed, Rosemary, Tarragon, Thyme, Extra Virgin Olive, Virgin Olive, Pure Olive, Pomace, Corn.

Pastas: Spaghetti, Fusilli, Fettuccine, Lasagna, Penne, Bucatini, Cannelloni, Cappelletti, Macaroni, Mafalde, Vermicelli, Gnocchi, Linguine, Tubetti, Ravioli.

Noodles: Rice, Vermicelli, Fettuccine, Udon, Glass, Spaghetti, Phad-Thai.

Fruits: Strawberry Tree, Sea Grape, American Mayapple, Queen Pineapple, Babacos, Blackberry, Blackcurrant, Blueberry, Carambola, Cranberry, Curuba, Dragon Fruit, Pithaya, Durian, Feijoas, Fig, Gooseberry, Grapefruit, Grenadilla, Kaffir Lime, Kiwifruit, Kumquat, Longan, Mangosteen, Passion Fruit, Pomelo, Persimmon, Redcurrant, Raspberry, Rambutan, Ugli Fruit, Thai Litchi, Peaches, Tamarind, Plum.

Vegetables: Broccoli, Brussels Sprout, Chinese Broccoli, Oriental Mustard, Malabar Gourd, Drumstick, Lolo Rosso, Frisse, Asparagus, Avocado, Celery, Artichoke, Cherry Tomato, Sweet Corn, Zucchini, Snow Pea, Pepper, Radicchio, Leek, Fennel, Chinese Cabbage, Pok-Choi, Chicory.

Sauces: Béchamel, Hollandaise, Vinaigrette, Albert, Alfredo, Aurore, Barbecue, Bernaise, Brown, Choron, Cocktail, Colbert, Cranberry, Crème Anglaise, Diable, Hoisin, Oyster, Parisienne, Piquante, Plum, Puttanesca, Romesco, Rouille, Tabasco, Verte, Worcestershire, White.

Syrups: Grain, Birch,Maple, Flower, Berry, Corn, Palm/Date, Golden, Black Treacle, Dark, Molasses, Fruit.

Herbs: Angelica, Basil, Bay, Chervil, Chives, Dill, Fennel, Lemongrass, Marjoram, Oregano, Mint, Parsley, Rosemary, Sage, Tarragon, Thyme.

Sea Food (Canned) : Prawn, Lobster, Squid, Red Snapper, Pomfret, Crab, Shrimp, Octopus, Oyster, Fish.

Cheese: Camembert, Cheddar, Colby, Wellington, Stilton, Feta, Gorgonzola, Emmental, Gouda, Edam, Gruye're, Havarti, Limburger, Mascarpone, Mozzarella, Parmesan, Romano, Fondue Cheese, Gruyezer Cheese, Ementhela Cheese, Ricotta, Roquefort, Swiss.

Mushroom (Canned): Button, Oyster, Sliced.

Miscellaneous Products: Yeast Extract, Spanish Saffron.

Meat Products: Mortadella, Parma Ham, Pancetta, White Penkin, Chicken Sausage, Chicken Frankfurter.

Lucky

10am to 8pm

120, INA Market, New Delhi, Ph: 24624550, 24631537

Oils: Canola, Flax Seed, Safflower, Tarragon, Extra Virgin Olive, Virgin Olive, Pure Olive, Pomace Olive, Corn.

Pastas: Spaghetti, Fusilli, Fettuccine, Lasagna, Penne, Cannelloni, Cappelletti, Macaroni, Vermicelli, Gnocchi, Linguine, Ravioli.

Noodles: Rice, Vermicelli, Fettuccine, Udon, Glass, Spaghetti, Phad-Thai.

Sauces: Bechamel, Vinaigrett, Barbecue, Cranberry, Hoisin, Oyste, Plum, Shrimp, Tobascco, Worcestershire, White Sauce.

Herbs: Angelica, Basil, Bay, Chervil, Chives, Dill, Fennel, Lemongrass, Marjoram, Oregano, Mint, Parsley, Rosemary, Sage, Tarragon, Thyme.

Sea Food (Frozen): Prawn, King Prawn, Lobster, Squid, Pomfret, Red Snapper, Crab, Shrimp, Octopus, Oyster, Fish.

Cheese: Camembert, Cheddar, Feta, Gorgonzola, Emmental, Gouda, Edam, Gruye're, Havarti, Mascarpone, Mozzarella, Parmesan, Romano, Ricotta, Roquefort, Swiss.

Mushrooms: Button/White, Chestnut, Cepes, Oyster, Enokitake, Shiitake, Matsutake, Truffle (White/Black), Morel, Paddy/Straw.

Flour: Italian, Rice.

Meat Products: Duck, Cornfed Chicken, Pork, Bacon, Ham, Salami, Sausage, Frankfurter, Lamb Rack.

Malik

AC

10am to 10pm

44, Defence Colony Market, New Delhi, Ph: 24333602, 24333735

Oils: Extra Virgin Olive, Virgin Olive, Pure Olive, Pomace Olive.

Pastas: Spaghetti, Fusilli, Fettuccine, Lasagna, Penne, Bucatini, Cannelloni, Cappelletti, Macaroni, Mafalde, Vermicelli.

Noodles: Rice, Vermicelli, Fettuccine, Glass, Spaghetti.

Sauces: Barbecue, Brown, Cranberry, Hoisin, Oyster, Plum, Tabasco, Worcestershire, White, Teriyaki, Stir Fry, Pesto, Black Pepper, Black Bean.

Syrups: Birch, Maple, Golden, Cocktail, Mocktail.

Herbs: Angelica, Basil, Bay, Chervil, Chives, Dill, Fennel,

Lemongrass, Marjoram, Oregano, Mint, Parsley, Rosemary, Sage, Tarragon, Thyme.

Sea Food: Prawn, Tiger Jumbo Prawn, Medium Prawn, Crab, Shrimp, Fish.

Cheese: Camembert, Cheddar, Feta, Gorgonzola, Emmental, Gouda, Edam, Gruye're, Havarti, Mozzarella, Parmesan, Romano, Ricotta, Roquefort, Swiss.

Miscellaneous Products: Tofu, Olive, Salad Dressing.

Modern Bazar

AC 10am to 9pm

18 B, Basant Lok Community Centre, Vasant Vihar, New Delhi, Ph: 41669777, 9891129999

Oils: Argan, Avocado, Canola/Rapeseed, Flax Seed, Hemp Seed, Macadamia, Palm Kernel, Rice Bran, Safflower, Tea Oil, Lime, Walnut, Watermelon, Dill Seed, Rosemary, Tarragon, Thyme, Extra Virgin Olive, Virgin Olive, Pure Olive, Pomace Olive, Corn.

Food Additives: Preservatives, Colour Additives, Flavour Enhancers, Emulsifiers, Stabilisers, Binders, Texturisers, Firming Agents, Dough Strengtheners, Conditioners, Sweeteners, Acidity Regulators, Leavening Agents, Anti-Caking Agents, Humectants, Thickeners, Colour Fixatives.

Pastas: Spaghetti, Fusilli, Fettuccine, Lasagna, Penne, Bucatini, Cannelloni, Cappelletti, Macaroni, Mafalde, Vermicelli, Gnocchi, Linguine, Tubetti, Ravioli.

Noodles: Rice, Vermicelli, Fettuccine, Udon, Glass, Spaghetti, Phad-Thai.

Fruits: Strawberry Tree, Sea Grape, American Mayapple, Queen Pineapple, Babacos, Blackberry, Blackcurrant, Blueberry, Carambola, Cranberry, Curuba, Dragon Fruit, Pithaya, Durian, Feijoas, Fig, Gooseberry, Grapefruit, Grenadilla, Kaffir Lime, Kiwifruit, Kumquat, Longan, Mangosteen, Passion Fruit, Pomelo, Persimmon, Redcurrant, Raspberry, Rambutan, Ugli Fruit, Thai Litchi, Peach, Tamarind, Plum.

Vegetables: Broccoli, Brussels Sprout, Chinese Broccoli, Oriental Mustard, Malabar Gourd, Drumstick, Lolo Rosso, Frisse, Asparagus, Avocado, Celery, Artichoke, Cherry Tomatoes, Sweet Corn, Zucchini, Snow Pea, Peppers, Radicchio, Leeks, Fennel, Chinese Cabbage,Pak-Choi, Chicory.

Sauces: Espagnole, Vinaigrette, Albert, Alfredo, Allemande, Aurore, Barbecue, Bernaise, Bercy, Brown, Choron, Cocktail, Colbert, Cranberry, Crème Anglaise, Hard, Harisse, Louis, Marguery, Marinara, Melba, Mornay, Newburg, Normande, Oyster, Piquante, Plum,Shrims, Sofrito, Tabasco, Worcestershire, White.

Syrups: Grain, Birch, Maple, Flower (Rose/Black/Locust), Berry, Corn, Palm/Date, Golden, Black Treacle, Dark, Molasses, Fruit.

Herbs: Angelica, Basil, Bay, Chervil, Chives, Dill, Fennel, Lemongrass, Marjoram, Oregano, Mint, Parsley, Rosemary, Sage, Tarragon, Thyme.

Sea Food (Frozen): Prawn, Tiger Jumbo Prawn, King Prawn, Lobster, Squid, Pomfret, Red Snaper, Crab, Shrimp, Octopus, Oyster, Fish.

Cheese: Camembert, Cheddar, Colby, Wellington, Stilton, Feta, Gorgonzola, Emmental, Gouda, Edam,

Gruye're, Havarti, Limburger, Mascarpone, Mozzarella, Parmesan, Romano, Ricotta, Roquefort, Swiss.

Mushrooms: Button/White, Chestnut, Chanterelle, Cepes, Oyster, Shiitake, Matsutake, Truffle(White/Black), Morel, Paddy/Straw, Wild Forest, Fairy Ring, Gucchi.

Miscellaneous Products: Jalepenos, 13 types of Olives, Cake ingredients, Yeast.

Meat Products: Duck, Turkey, Cornfed Chicken, Pork, Bacon, Quail, Pancetta, Ham, Salami, Sausage, Frankfurter, Lamb Rack.

Morning Store

AC 9am to 9pm

M 41, Greater Kailash I Market, New Delhi, Ph: 29244318, 29231694, 41734833

Bimal International, 2, CSC, Sector B 1, Vasant Kunj, New Delhi, Ph: 26893571, 20256271

Oils: Canola, Flax Seed, Extra Virgin Olive, Virgin Olive, Pure Olive, Pomace Olive, Corn.

Food Additives: Preservatives, Colour Additives, Flavour Enhancers, Emulsifiers, Stabilisers, Thickeners, Binders, Texturisers, Firming Agents, Dough Strengtheners, Conditioners, Sweeteners, Acidity Regulators, Leavening Agents, Anti-Caking Agents, Humectant, Colour Fixatives.

Pastas: Spaghetti, Fusilli, Fettuccine, Lasagna, Penne, Bucatini, Cannelloni, Cappelletti, Macaroni, Mafalde, Vermicelli, Gnocchi, Linguine, Tubetti, Ravioli.

Noodles: Rice, Vermicelli, Fettuccine.

Fruits: Strawberry Tree, Sea Grape, American Mayapple, Queen Pineapple, Babacos, Blackberry, Blackcurrant, Blueberry, Carambola, Cranberry, Curuba, Dragon Fruit, Pithaya, Durian, Feijoas, Fig, Gooseberry, Grapefruit, Grenadilla, Kaffir Lime, Kiwifruit, Kumquat, Longan, Mangosteen, Passion Fruit, Pomelo, Persimmon, Redcurrant, Raspberry, Rambutan, Ugli Fruit, Thai Litchi, Peach, Tamarind, Plum.

Sauces: Hollandaise, Vinaigrette, Alfredo, Barbecue, Bernaise, Bercy, Bordelaise, Cocktail, Colbert, Cranberry, Crème Anglaise, Figaro, Harissa, Hoisin, Mornay, Newburg, Normande, Oyster, Parisienne, Piquante, Plum, Shrims, Tabasco, Verte, Worcestershire, White.

Syrups: Grain, Birch, Maple, Flower (Rose/Black/Locust), Berry, Corn, Palm/Date, Golden, Black Treacle, Dark, Molasses, Fruit, Cocktail, Mocktail.

Herbs: Angelica, Basil, Bay, Chervil, Chives, Dill, Fennel, Lemongrass, Marjoram, Oregano, Mint, Parsley, Rosemary, Sage, Tarragon, Thyme.

Sea Food (Canned): Prawn, Lobster, Crab, Shrimp, Octopus, Oyster, Fish.

Cheese: Camembert, Cheddar, Colby, Stilton, Feta, Gorgonzola, Emmental, Gouda, Edam, Mascarpone, Mozzarella, Parmesan, Romano Ricotta, Roquefort, Swiss.

Mushrooms: Button, Oyster, Shiitake, Morel.

Flour: Arrowroot, Buckwheat, Chickpea, Maize Meal, Semolina.

Meat Products (Canned): Ham, Bacon, Salami, Sausage.

Navdanya

10am to 9pm

- 18 Dilli Haat, New Delhi, Ph: 65343067
- E 52, Hauz Khas, New Delhi, Ph: 26854069, 40793565

Oil (Organic): Mustard, Linseed, Sesame, Olive, Peanut.

Noodles (Organic): Rice, Fettuccine, Spaghetti.

Herbs (Organic): Angelica, Basil, Bay, Chervil, Chives, Dill, Fennel, Lemongrass, Marjoram, Oregano, Mint, Parsley, Rosemary, Sage, Tarragon, Thyme, Artemesia, Kalmegh.

Grains (Organic): Wheat Basket, Millet Powder Foxtail Millet, Finger Millet, Barnyard Millet, Buck Wheat Millet, Pearl Millet, Amaranth.

Pulses (Organic): Special Navrangi Dal, White Rajma.

Miscellaneous Products: Natural Sweetner (Steve).

Spices (Organic): Cumin, Fenugreek, Coriander, Turmeric, Chilli.

Seeds (Organic): Mustard Seeds, Sun Greek Seeds.

New Anand

SS 9.30am to 8pm

- 110, INA Market, New Delhi, Ph: 24611917, 9811560180

Oils: Rapeseed, Macadamia, Palm Kernel, Rosemary, Tarragon, Thyme, Extra Virgin Olive, Virgin Olive, Pure Olive, Pomace Olive, Corn.

Pastas: Spaghetti, Fusilli, Fettuccine, Lasagna, Penne, Bucatini, Cannelloni, Cappelletti, Macaroni, Mafalde, Vermicelli, Gnocchi, Linguine, Tubetti, Ravioli.

Sauces: Barbecue, Cocktail, Colbert, Cranberry , Oyster, Plum, Tabasco, Verte, Worcestershire, White.

Syrups: Grain, Maple, Flower (Rose/Black/Locust), Berry, Corn, Palm/Date, Golden, Black Treacle, Dark, Molasses, Fruit.

Herbs: Angelica, Basil, Bay, Chervil, Chives, Dill, Fennel, Lemongrass, Marjoram, Oregano, Mint, Parsley, Rosemary, Sage, Tarragon, Thyme.

Cheese: Camembert, Cheddar, Colby, Wellington, Stilton, Feta, Gorgonzola, Emmental, Gouda, Edam, Gruye're, Havarti, Limburger, Mascarpone, Mozzarella, Parmesan, Romano, Ricotta, Roquefort, Swiss.

Mushrooms: Button/White, Chestnut, Chanterelle, Cepes, Oyster, Enokitake, Shiitake, Matsutake, Truffle(White/Black), Morel, Paddy/Straw.

Om The Super Market

AC SS 10am to 10pm

- B 165, Gujranwalan Town Part 1, Delhi, Ph: 9891111223, 9811061816, 27413963

Oils: Argan, Canola/ Rapeseed, Rice Bran, Safflower, Tea Oil, Extra Virgin Olive, Virgin Olive, Pure Olive, Pomace Olive , Corn.

Food Additives: Preservatives, Colour Additives, Sweeteners.

Pastas: Spaghetti, Fusilli, Fettuccine, Lasagna, Penne, Bucatini, Cannelloni, Cappelletti, Macaroni, Mafalde, Vermicelli, Gnocchi, Linguine, Tubetti, Ravioli.

Sauces: Vinaigrette (Oil, Vinegar combinations), Barbecue, Brown, Cocktail, Cranberry, Crème Anglaise, Figaro, Harissa, Hoisin, Oyster, Plum, Shrimp, Tabasco, Worcestershire, White Sauce.

Syrups: Grain, Birch, Maple, Flower Syrup (Rose/Black/ Locust), Berry, Corn, Palm/Date, Golden, Black Treacle, Dark, Molasses, Fruit.

Herbs: Angelica, Basil, Bay, Chervil, Chives, Dill, Fennel, Lemongrass, Marjoram, Oregano, Mint, Parsley, Rosemary, Sage, Tarragon, Thyme, Artemesia, Kalmegh.

Cheese: Camembert, Cheddar, Colby, Gorgonzola, Emmental, Gouda, Edam, Mozzarella, Swiss.

Mushrooms: Button, Shiitake, Morel.

Miscellaneous Products: Baked Beans, French Fries, Dyna Bite, Smiley, Pasty, Tatar, American Corn.

Palkit Impex

9am to 7.30pm

■ **12-13, DDA Market, LSC, Maidan Gari, New Delhi, Ph: 9350530875, 29956143, 9818448620**

■ **C 82, Basement, Shiwalik, Malviya Ngr. New Delhi**

Noodles: Somen, Udon, Soba, Chasoba, Shishu Soba, Cup.

Sauces: Seasoning Mix, Soya, Mirin Sweetening, Tonkatsu, Grilled Meat, Kikkoman Cooking Sauce, Usukuchi Manpack Syoyu, Teriyaki, Yamasass, Koikuchi, Bulldog, Otafukuss.

Pastes: Soyabean, Shir Miso, Inaka Miso, Shinsyu Miso, Akamiso, Red Bean, Miso Ramen Soup Base.

Mushrooms: Shiitake Dried, Nameko Wet, Kanpyo Dried Gourd.

Seasoning Mix: Ebara Seasoning, Takara Seasoning, Soft Panko, Hondasi Hako, Kona Wasabi, Neri Wasabi, Kuro Goma Shiro, Shichimi, Chicken Bouillon, Neri Goma Shiro, Irigoma Shiro, Yamahide, Toban Jan, Karashi, Horseraddish.

Flour: Tempura, Potato Starch, Japanese Starch, Ohgon Tempura, Katakuriko Starch.

Sea Weed: Brown Argae, Wakame, Hidaka Kelp, Neri, Agar Agar, Green Leave, Kaneu Dried, Riken Dried, Shonaifu, Hanabishi Dried, Ito Katsuo.

Vinegar: Rice, Ponzu, Mitsukan Seasoning, Suehiro Su, Shiragikusu, Otafuku Seasoning, Sauce Vinegar.

Miscellaneous Products: Bamboo Shoot, Dried Gourd Shavings, Japanese Rice, Konnyaku Jelly, Bread Crumb, Seven Spice Mix, Chicken Bouillon, Bonito Flex.

Meat Products: Fish, Tuna.

Pick Fresh Fish

AC

10am to 10pm

■ **29/1, East Patel Nagar, New Delhi, Ph: 9811022247, 42480477/55**

Sea Food: Prawn, Tiger Jumbo Prawn, King Prawn, Lobsters, Squid, Pomfret, Red Snappers, Crab, Shrimp, Octopus, Oyster, Fish.

Meat Products: Duck, Turkey, Cornfed Chicken, Pork, Bacon, Quail, Pancetta, Ham, Salami, Sausage, Frankfurter, Lamb Rack.

Pigpo

11.30am to 7pm

- 5, Shanti Niketan Market, New Delhi, Ph: 24115335
- 9, Jor Bagh Market, New Delhi, Ph: 24611723, 24626930
- 22, Community Centre, New Friends Colony, New Delhi

Meat Products: Fresh Pork- Without Skin, Chop, Fillet, Minae, Spare Rib, Sausage, Fresh Bacon Slice, Fresh Smoked Pork, Chicken Frankfurter, Smoked Chicken, Ham, Pork Salami, Pork Frankfurter, Pork Smoked Sausage, Pork Seekh Kabab, Chicken Ham, Chicken Salami, Chicken Sausage.

Pindi Fruit Mart

9am to 9pm

- 28 A, Defence Colony Market, New Delhi Ph: 41552530, 24333593

Oils: Avocado, Lime, Extra Virgin, Virgin Olive, Pure Olive, Pomace Olive.

Noodles: Rice Noodles.

Fruits: Strawberry Tree, Sea Grape, American Mayapple, Queen Pineapple, Babacos, Blackberry, Blackcurrant, Blueberry, Carambola, Cranberry, Curuba, Dragon Fruit, Pithaya, Durian, Feijoas, Fig, Gooseberry, Grape fruit, Grenadilla, Kaffir Lime, Honey Melon, Rock Melon, Williams Pears, Kiwifruit, Kumquat, Longan, Mangosteen, Passion Fruit, Pomelo, Persimmon, Thal Guava, Hawaian Papaya, Kenya Banana, Redcurrant, Raspberry, Rambutan, Ugli Fruit, Thai Litchi, Peach, Tamarind, Plum.

Vegetables: Broccoli, Brussels Sprout, Chinese Broccoli, Oriental Mustard, Malabar Gourd, Drumstick, Rocket (Arugla Leaves), Thai Ginger (Galangle), Lolo Rosso, Frisse, Asparagus, Avocado, Celery, Artichoke, Cherry Tomato, Sweet Corn, Zucchini, Snow Pea, Pepper, Radicchio, Leek, Fennel, Chinese Cabbage, Pok-Choi, Chicory, Bean Sprout, Bamboo Shoot, White Onion.

Herbs: Angelica, Basil, Bay, Chervil, Chives, Dill, Fennel, Lemongrass, Marjoram, Oregano, Mint, Parsley, Rosemary, Sage, Tarragon, Thyme.

Pioneer

10am to 6pm

- B 84/4, Jeewan Park, Pankha Road, New Delhi, Ph: 9811535370

Cheese: Pizza, Processed Cheddar, Mozzarella, Processed Slice, Cheese Spread, Flavoured Cheese (Garlic, Onion, Jeera).

Prakash

10.30am to 7.30pm

- G 1, Hemkund Chamber 89, Nehru Place, New Delhi, Ph: 26220038, 26433231

Oils: Extra Virgin Olive, Virgin Olive, Pure Olive, Pomace Olive, Corn.

Pastas: Spaghetti, Fusilli, Fettuccini, Lasagna, Penne, Bucatini, Cannelloni, Cappelletti, Macaroni, Mafalde, Vermicelli,

Gnocchi, Linguine, Tubetti, Ravioli.

Noodles: Rice, Vermicelli, Fettuccine.

Rahul

9am to 7pm

A 64, Rajendra Park Extention, Lane 3, Nangaloi, Delhi, Ph: 9811530329, 25942166

Oils: Almond, Sesame.

Food Additives: Preservatives, Colour Additives, Sweeteners.

Pastas: Spaghetti, Fusilli, Fettuccine, Lasagne, Penne, Bucatini, Cannelloni, Cappelletti, Macaroni, Mafalde, Vermicelli, Ravioli.

Noodles: Udon, Shoba.

Sauces: Barbecue, Cranberry, Crème Anglaise, Diable, Figaro, Genevoise, Hard, Harissa, Hoisin, Louis, Marinara, Melba, Oyster, Parisienne, Piquante, Plum, Puttanesca, Shrimp, Sofrito, Tabasco, Worcestershire, White.

Syrups: Grain, Birch, Maple, Flower (Rose/Black/Locust), Berry, Corn, Palm/Date, Golden, Black Treacle, Dark, Molasses, Fruit.

Herbs: Angelica, Basil, Bay, Chervil, Chives, Dill, Fennel, Lemongrass, Marjoram, Oregano, Mint, Parsley, Rosemary, Sage, Tarragon, Thyme.

Cheese: Camembert, Cheddar, Colby, Wellington, Stilton, Feta, Gorgonzola, Emmental, Gouda, Edam, Gruye're, Havarti, Limburger, Mascarpone, Mozzarella, Parmesan, Romano, Ricotta, Roquefort, Swiss.

Mushrooms: Button/White, Chestnut, Oyster, Shiitake, Matsutake, Morel, Paddy/Straw.

Miscellaneous Products: Sushi Rice, Nori Sheet, Wasbi Powder, Hondshi Powder, Miso Paste, Tempura Flower, other ingredients used in Thai, Italian, Japanese, Chinese Cuisine.

Rajasthan

AC

9.30am to 9.30pm

S 9/2, Green Park, New Delhi, Ph: 26515414, 26866025

Oils: Extra Virgin Olive,Virgin Olive, Pure Olive, Pomace Olive.

Pastas: Spaghetti, Fusilli, Fettuccine, Lasagne, Penne, Bucatini, Cannelloni, Cappelletti, Macaroni, Mafalde, Vermicelli, Ravioli.

Sauces: Albert, Barbecue, Bercy, Bigarade, Bor Brown, Choron, Cocktail, Colbert, Cranberry, Crème Anglaise, Figaro, Hard, Harissa, Hoisin, Marinara, Oyster, Plum, Shrimp, Sofrito, Tabasco, Verte, Worcestershire, White.

Syrups: Grain, Birch, Maple, Flower (Rose/Black/Locust), Berry, Corn, Palm/Date, Golden, Black Treacle, Dark Syrup, Molasses, Fruit Syrups.

Herbs: Angelica, Basil, Bay, Chervil, Chives, Dill, Fennel, Lemongrass, Marjoram, Oregano, Mint, Parsley, Rosemary, Sage, Tarragon, Thyme.

Cheese: Camembert, Cheddar, Colby, Stilton, Feta, Gorgonzola, Gouda, Edam, Mozzarella, Parmesan, Romano, Ricotta.

Flour: Arrowroot, Buckwheat, Chickpea, Maize meal, Semolina.

Republic of Chicken

AC 🏠 SS
11am to 11pm

- Delivery: 1800-103-1033
- Ground Floor, Lila Ram Market, Masjid Moth, New Delhi, Ph: 46033831
- Silver Oaks Aptts, DLF Phase I, Gurgaon, Ph: 124-4279161
- E-2/2, Shopping Centre, Alaknanda, New Delhi, Ph: 40523818
- Ground Floor, CC Market, Shalimar Bagh, Delhi, Ph: 27496465
- 1/51, West Punjabi Bagh, New Delhi, Ph: 45074319
- AB-12, Ground Floor, Community Centre, Safdarjung Enclave, New Delhi, Ph: 46024817
- G-10, Hauz Khas, New Delhi, Ph: 46067625
- C-4, Malviya Nagar, New Delhi, Ph: 40529724
- 12 & 13, DDA Market No. 2, CR Park, New Delhi, Ph: 40586504
- 8, Om Shubham Tower, Neelam Bata Road, Faridabad, Ph: 0129-4035945

Khubchand and Pigpo are the very distant country cousins of this smart, sleek set of processed chicken stores. Chicken in all its avatars is what you get here, but far from being sold loose, the birds, reportedly bred in the company's own plant near Ropar, are fed with a carefully controlled feed that makes their flesh tender and non-stringy when cooked. The delicatessen offers packaged Chicken Meat Loaf, Smoked Chicken Breast, Chicken Dimsum, Chicken Tikkas, Bread-crumbed Chicken Nuggets and a whole host of other processed chicken products. The vegetarian option is limited to dim sums, but chicken products include Ajwain Seekh Kabab, Chicken Frankfurter Hot Dog and Chicken Seekh Kabab Hot Dog. All the products are either ready to eat or ready to cook and make a healthy option to store in your deep freeze or to carry with you on a long journey. You can also have a few items baked or steamed inside the store to eat on the spot.

S K Store

🏠 SS
10am to 8pm

- 111-112, INA Market, New Delhi, Ph: 24631537, 24627383, 9811560125

Oils: Canola, Flax Seed, Safflower, Tarragon, Extra Virgin Olive, Virgin Olive, Pure Olive, Pomace Olive, Corn.

Pastas: Spaghetti, Fusilli, Fettuccine, Lasagne, Penne, Cannelloni, Cappelletti, Macaroni, Vermicelli, Gnocchi, Linguine, Ravioli.

Sauces: Bechamel, Vinaigrette, Barbecue, Cranberry, Hoisin, Oyster, Plum, Shrimp, Tabasco, Worcestershire, White.

Herbs: Angelica, Basil, Bay, Chervil, Chives, Dill, Fennel, Lemongrass, Marjoram, Oregano, Mint, Parsley, Rosemary, Sage, Tarragon, Thyme.

Cheese: Camembert, Cheddar, Feta, Gorgonzola, Emmental, Gouda, Edam, Gruye're, Havarti, Mascarpone, Mozzarella, Parmesan, Romano, Ricotta, Roquefort, Swiss.

Mushrooms: Button/White, Chestnut, Cepe, Oyster, Enokitake, Shiitake, Matsutake, Truffle (White/Black), Morel, Paddy/Straw.

S Naresh Kumar

AC | Card | Home delivery
10am to 7pm

D Block, 397, Near Sabzi Mandi, Azadpur, Delhi, Ph: 9811786678

Fruits: Strawberry Tree, Sea Grape, American Mayapple, Queen Pineapple, Babacos, Blackberry, Blackcurrant, Blueberry, Carambola, Cranberry, Curuba, Dragon Fruit, Pithaya, Durian, Feijoas, Fig, Gooseberry, Grapefruit, Grenadilla, Kaffir Lime, Kiwifruit, Kumquat, Longan, Mangosteen, Passion Fruit, Pomelo, Persimmon, Redcurrant, Raspberry, Rambutan, Ugli Fruit, Thai Litchi, Peaches, Tamarind, Plum.

Vegetables: Broccoli, Brussels Sprout, Chinese Broccoli, Oriental Mustard, Malabar Gourd, Drumstick, Lolo Rosso, Frisse, Asparagus, Avocado, Celery, Artichoke, Cherry Tomato, Sweet Corn.

Sabji Kendra

AC | Card | Home delivery
8.30am to 9pm

9 AB, Taimoor Nagar, New Friends Colony, New Delhi, Ph: 65697793, 65694861, 65697792, 94

Fruits: Strawberry Tree, Sea Grape, American Mayapple, Queen Pineapple, Babacos, Blackberry, Blackcurrant, Blueberry, Carambola, Cranberry, Curuba, Dragon Fruit, Pithaya, Durian, Feijoas, Fig, Gooseberry, Grapefruit, Grenadilla, Kaffir Lime, Kiwifruit, Kumquat, Longan, Mangosteen, Passion Fruit, Pomelo, Persimmon, Redcurrant, Raspberry, Rambutan, Ugli Fruit, Thai Litchi, Peach, Tamarind, Plum.

Vegetables: Broccoli, Brussels Sprout, Chinese Broccoli, Oriental Mustard, Malabar Gourd, Drumstick, Lolo Rosso, Frisse, Asparagus, Avocado, Celery, Artichoke, Cherry Tomatoes, Sweet Corn, Zucchini, Snow Pea, Pepper, Radicchio, Leek, Fennel, Chinese Cabbage, Pok-Choi, Chicory, Baby Carrot, Baby Corn, Bamboo Shoot, Fresh Basil, Beans Sprout, Dill Soya Endive, Iceberg Lettuce, Leeks, Lemon Leaf, Fresh Oyster, Fresh Parsley, Romain Lettuce, Thai Ginger.

Sauces: Bechamel, Vinaigrette, Barbecue, Cranberry, Hoisin, Oyster, Plum, Shrimp, Tobascco, Worcestershire, White Sauce.

Sachdeva Vegetable and Fruits

Card | Home delivery
9am to 9pm

183, INA Market, New Delhi, Ph: 24636041, 24603517

Pastas: Spaghetti, Fusilli, Fettuccine, Lasagna, Penne, Macaroni.

Fruits: Strawberry Tree, Sea Grape, American Mayapple, Queen Pineapple, Babacos, Blackberry, Blackcurrant, Blueberry, Carambola, Cranberry, Curuba, Dragon Fruit, Pithaya, Durian, Feijoas, Fig, Gooseberry, Grapefruit, Grenadilla, Kaffir Lime, Kiwifruit, Kumquat, Longan, Mangosteen, Passion Fruit, Pomelo, Persimmon, Redcurrant, Raspberry, Rambutan, Ugli Fruit, Thai Litchi, Tamarind, Plum.

Vegetables: Broccoli, Brussel Sprout, Chinese Broccoli, Oriental Mustard, Malabar Gourd, Drumstick, Baby Corn, American Sweet Corn, Red Radish, Lolo Rosso, Frisse, Asparagus,

Avocado, Celery, Artichoke, Cherry Tomato, Sweet Corn, Zucchini, Snow Pea, Pepper, Radicchio, Leek, Fennel, Chinese Cabbage, Pok-Choi, Chicory, Thai Ginger, Thai Lemongrass, Thai Basil, Bamboo Shoot, White Onion, Baby Onion.

Herbs: Angelica, Basil, Bay, Chervil, Chives, Dill, Fennel, Lemongrass, Marjoram, Oregano, Mint, Parsley, Rosemary, Sage, Tarragon, Thyme.

Sethi Fruits and Vegetable

AC SS
8.30am to 9pm

119, INA Market, New Delhi, Ph: 24692517

Fruits: Strawberry Tree, Sea Grape, American Mayapple, Queen Pineapple, Babacos, Blackberry, Blackcurrant, Grapefruit, Kiwifruit, Passion Fruit, Pomelo, Thai Litchi, Peach, Tamarind, Plum.

Herbs: Angelica, Basil, Bay, Chervil, Chives, Dill, Fennel, Lemongrass, Marjoram, Oregano, Mint, Parsley, Rosemary, Sage, Tarragon, Thyme.

Mushrooms: Button/White, Chestnut, Oyster, Enokitake, Shiitake, Morels.

Pastas: Spaghetti, Fusilli, Fettuccini, Lasagna, Penne, Macaroni.

Vegetables: Broccoli, Brussels Sprout, Chinese Broccoli, Oriental Mustard, Malabar Gourd, Drumstick, Lolo Rosso, Frisse, Asparagus, Avocado, Celery, Artichoke, Cherry Tomato, Sweet Corn, Zucchini, Snow Pea, Pepper, Radicchio, Leek, Fennel, Chinese Cabbage, Pak-Choi, Chicory.

Sharda

AC SS
9am to 8:30pm

71 B, Khan Market, New Delhi, Ph: 24693519

Oils: Flax Seed, Dill Seed, Rosemary, Tarragon, Extra Virgin Olive, Virgin Olive, Pure Olive, Pomace Olive, Corn.

Pastas: Spaghetti, Fusilli, Fettuccine, Lasagna, Penne, Macaroni.

Fruits (Canned): Cape Gooseberry, Blackberry.

Sauces: Barbecue, Brown, Choron, Cocktail, Colbert, Cranberry, Crème Anglaise, Figaro, Hard, Harissa, Hoisin, Louis, Marinara, Oyster, Plum, Shrimp, Tabasco, Verte, Worcestershire, White.

Syrups: Grain, Birch, Maple, Flower (Rose/Black/Locust), Berry, Corn, Palm/Date, Golden, Dark, Fruit.

Herbs: Angelica, Basil, Bay, Chervil, Chives, Dill, Fennel, Lemongrass, Marjoram, Oregano, Mint, Parsley, Rosemary, Sage, Tarragon, Thyme.

Sea Food: Canned Fish

Cheese: Camembert, Cheddar, Colby, Stilton, Feta, Gorgonzola, Emmental, Gouda, Edam, Havarti, Mozzarella.

Miscellaneous Products: Flavoured Tea (Kashmiri Kawa Tea, Jasmine), Olive, Guava Jelly.

Shell Overseas

AC
9am to 6.30pm

D 3/1, Rana Pratap Bagh, Delhi, Ph: 27414787, 27438031, 9350257100

Chocolates, Bakery Ingredients: Chocolate Slab, Chocolate Mould, Chocolate Paper, Chocolate Cup, Chocolate Flavour, Fruits filling for Chocolate, Nuts, Cocoa Powder, Chocolate Paste, Icing Sugar, Jelly, Bread Improver, Sorbic Acid, Sorbic Potassium.

Shiv Fruit Mart

AC SS 8am to 8.30pm

17, Bengali Market, New Delhi, Ph: 23352380

Fruits: Strawberry Tree, Sea Grape, American Mayapple, Queen Pineapple, Babacos, Blackberry, Blackcurrant, Blueberry, Carambola, Cranberry, Curuba, Dragon Fruit, Pithaya, Durian, Feijoas, Fig, Gooseberry, Grapefruit, Grenadilla, Kaffir Lime, Kiwifruit, Kumquat, Longan, Mangosteen, Passion Fruit, Pomelo, Persimmon, Redcurrant, Raspberry, Rambutan, Ugli Fruit, Thai Litchi, Peach, Tamarind, Plum.

Vegetable: Broccoli, Brussels Sprout, Chinese Broccoli, Oriental Mustard, Malabar Gourd, Drumstick, Lolo Rosso, Frisse, Asparagus, Avocado, Celery, Artichoke, Cherry Tomato, Sweet Corn, Zucchini, Snow Pea, Pepper, Radicchio, Leek, Fennel, Chinese Cabbage, Pok-Choi, Chicory.

Shri Morning Palace

9am to 9pm

E 44/B, Hauz Khas, Main Market, New Delhi, Ph: 41655071, 26965252, 26565352

Oils: Canola/Rapeseed, Flax Seed, Safflower, Tea Oil, Extra Virgin Olive, Virgin Olive, Pure Olive, Pomace Olive.

Food Additives: Preservatives, Colour Additives, Sweeteners.

Pastas: Spaghetti, Fusilli, Fettuccine, Lasagna, Penne, Bucatini, Cannelloni, Cappelletti, Macaroni, Mafalde, Vermicelli, Gnocchi, Linguine, Tubetti, Ravioli.

Sauces: Vinaigrette, Barbecue, Brown, Cocktail, Cranberry, Oyster, Plum, Tabasco, Worcestershire, White.

Syrups: Maple, Golden, Fruit Syrup.

Herbs: Angelica, Basil, Bay, Chervil, Chives, Dill, Fennel, Lemongrass, Marjoram, Oregano, Mint, Parsley, Rosemary, Sage, Tarragon, Thyme.

Sea Food: Tuna, Mackerel, Sardine.

Cheese: Camembert, Cheddar, Colby, Wellington, Stilton, Feta, Gorgonzola, Emmental, Gouda, Edam, Gruye're, Havarti, Mozzarella, Parmesan, Ricotta, Swiss.

Flour: Semolina, Buckwheat.

Shri Sant Lal Ramji Dass

9am to 9pm

E 44/A, Hauz Khas, Main Market, New Delhi, Ph: 26569042, 26855796, 9810145545, 9891939793

Oils: Canola, Rice Bran, Extra Virgin Olive, Virgin Olive, Pure Olive, Pomace Olive, Corn.

Food Additives: Sweetners.

Pastas: Spaghetti, Fusilli, Fettuccine, Lasagne, Penne, Cannelloni, Vermicelli.

Sauces: Barbecue, Hoisin, Oyster, Tabasco, Worcestershire Sauce

Syrups: Birch, Maple, Corn, Golden.

Herbs: Angelica, Basil, Bay, Chervil, Chives, Dill, Fennel, Lemongrass, Marjoram, Oregano, Mint, Parsley, Rosemary, Sage, Tarragon, Thyme.

Cheese: Camembert, Cheddar, Feta, Emmental, Gouda, Adam, Havarti, Mozzarella, Parmesan.

Star Bazaar

10am to 10pm

HS 10, Kailash Colony Market, Kailash Colony, New Delhi, Ph: 9871744264, 41635434

Oils: Argan, Avocado, Canola/Rapeseed, Flax Seed, Hemp Seed, Macadamia, Palm Kernel, Rice Bran, Safflower, Tea Oil, Walnut, Watermelon, Dill Seed, Rosemary, Tarragon, Thyme, Extra Virgin Olive, Virgin Olive, Pure Olive, Pomace Olive, Corn.

Food Additives: Preservatives, Colour Additives, Flavour Enhancers, Emulsifiers, Stabilisers, Thickeners, Binders, Texturisers, Firming Agents, Dough Strengtheners, Conditioners, Sweeteners, Acidity Regulators, Leavening Agents, Anti-Caking Agents, Humectants, Colour Fixatives.

Pastas: Spaghetti, Fusilli, Fettuccine, Lasagna, Penne, Bucatini, Cannelloni, Cappelletti, Macaroni, Mafalde, Vermicelli, Gnocchi, Linguine, Tubetti, Ravioli.

Noodles: Rice, Vermicelli, Fettuccine, Spaghetti, Glass, Udon.

Sauces: Espagnole, Velouté, Béchamel, Hollandaise, Vinaigrette, Albert, Alfredo, Allemande, Aurore, Barbecue, Bernaise, Bercy, Bigarade, Bordelaise, Brown, Chasseur, Choron, Cocktail, Colbert, Cranberry, Crème Anglaise, Diable, Figaro, Genevoise, Hard, Harissa, Hoisin, Louis, Lyonnaise, Maltaise, Marguery, Marinara, Melba, Mornay, Newburg, Normande, Oyster, Parisienne, Piquante, Plum, Puttanesca, Ranchero, Rémoulade, Romesco, Rouille, Sofrito, Tabasco, Verte, Worcestershire, White.

Syrups: Grain, Birch, Maple, Flower (Rose/Black/ Locust), Berry, Corn, Palm/Date, Golden, Black Treacle, Dark, Molasses, Fruit .

Herbs: Angelica, Basil, Bay, Chervil, Chives, Dill, Fennel, Lemongrass, Marjoram, Oregano, Mint, Parsley, Rosemary, Sage, Tarragon, Thyme.

Sea Food (Canned): Prawn, Tiger Jumbo Prawn, King Prawn, Lobster, Squid, Pomfret, Crab, Shrimp, Octopus.

Cheese: Camembert, Cheddar, Colby, Wellington, Stilton, Feta, Gorgonzola, Emmental, Gouda, Edam, Gruye're, Havarti, Limburger, Mascarpone, Mozzarella, Parmesan, Romano, Ricotta, Roquefort, Swiss.

Mushrooms: Button/White, Chestnut, Chanterelle, Cepes, Oyster, Enokitake, Shiitake, Matsutake, Truffle (White/Black), Morel, Paddy/Straw.

Miscellaneous Products: Jalapeno, Seaweed, Wasabi, Bean Curd, Tofu, Bamboo Shoot.

Meat Products (Canned): Cornfed Chicken, Pork, Bacon, Pancetta, Ham, Salami, Sausage, Frankfurter, Lamb Rack.

Steak House

9.30am to 7.30pm

13/8, Jor Bagh Market, New Delhi, Ph: 24611008, 24611129, 24658034, 24658037

Oils: Extra Virgin Olive, Virgin Olive, Pure Olive, Pomace Olive, Walnut, Tarragon, Thyme, Corn.

Food Additives: Sweeteners.

Pastas: Spaghetti, Fusilli, Fettuccine, Lasagna, Penne, Bucatini, Cannelloni, Cappelletti, Macaroni, Mafalde, Vermicelli, Gnocchi, Linguine, Tubetti, Ravioli.

Noodles: Vermicelli, Fettuccine, Spaghetti, Udon.

Sauces: Vinaigrette, Alfredo, Barbecue, Brown, Chasseur, Choron, Cocktail, Colbert, Cranberry, Crème Anglaise, Genevoise, Hoisin, Marinara, Oyster, Piquante, Plum, Puttanesca, Ranchero, Rémoulade, Shrims, Tabasco, Worcestershire, White sauces.

Syrups: Grain, Maple, Flower (Rose/Black/Locust), Berry, Corn, Palm/Date, Golden, Black Treacle, Molasses, Fruit.

Herbs: Angelica, Basil, Bay, Chervil, Chives, Dill, Fennel, Lemongrass, Marjoram, Oregano, Mint, Parsley, Rosemary, Sage, Tarragon, Thyme.

Sea Food: Prawn, Tiger Jumbo Prawn, King Prawn, Lobster, Squid, Pomfret, Red Snapper, Crab, Shrimp, Octopus, Fish.

Cheese: Camembert, Cheddar, Colby, Wellington, Stilton, Feta, Gorgonzola, Emmental, Gouda, Edam, Gruye're, Havarti, Mascarpone, Mozzarella, Parmesan, Romano, Ricotta, Roquefort, Swiss.

Mushrooms (Frozen): Cepes, Oyster, Shiitake.

Flour: Buckwheat, Tempura.

Meat Products (Canned): Duck, Turkey, Cornfed Chicken, Pork, Bacon, Ham, Salami, Sausage, Frankfurter, Lamb Rack.

Store 18 Noida

10am to 9.30pm

K 2, Somdutt Tower, Sector 18, Noida, Ph: 95120-2516931, 2516932

Oils: Extra Virgin Olive, Virgin Olive, Pure Olive, Pomace Olive, Flax Seed.

Food Additives: Preservatives, Colour Additives, Flavour Enhancers, Emulsifiers, Stabilisers, Thickeners, Binders, Texturisers, Firming Agents, Dough Strengtheners, Conditioners, Sweeteners, Acidity Regulators, Leavening Agents, Anti-Caking Agents, Humectants, Colour Fixatives.

Pastas: Spaghetti, Fusilli, Fettuccine, Lasagna, Penne, Bucatini, Cannelloni, Cappelletti, Macaroni, Mafalde, Vermicelli, Gnocchi, Linguine, Tubetti, Ravioli.

Noodles: Rice, Vermicelli, Fettuccine, Udon, Glass, Spaghetti, Phad-Thai.

Sauces: Barbecue, Bercy, Brown, Chasseur, Choron, Cocktail, Colbert, Cranberry, Crème Anglaise, Figaro, Hard Sauce, Harissa, Hoisin, Oyster, Plum, Romesco, Shrims, Tabasco, Verte, Worcestershire, White.

Syrups: Grain, Birch, Maple, Flower (Rose/Black/Locust), Berry, Corn, Palm/Date, Golden, Black Treacle, Dark, Molasses, Fruit.

Herbs: Angelica, Basil, Bay, Chervil, Chives, Dill, Fennel, Lemongrass, Marjoram, Oregano, Mint, Parsley, Rosemary, Sage, Tarragon, Thyme.

Sea Food: Prawn, Tiger

Jumbo Prawn, King Prawn, Lobster, Crab, Shrimp, Oyster, Fish.

Cheese: Camembert, Cheddar, Colby, Wellington, Stilton, Feta, Gorgonzola, Emmental, Gouda, Edam, Gruye're, Havarti, Limburger, Mascarpone, Mozzarella, Parmesan, Romano, Ricotta, Roquefort, Swiss.

Mushrooms: Button, Chestnut, Shiitake.

Miscellaneous Products: Olives.

Meat Products (Frozen): Salami, Seekh Kebab.

Suresh Kumar

AC SS

9.30 am to 6pm

A-17, Sonu Towers Second Floor, Dr. Mukherjee Nagar Commercial Complex, New Delhi, Ph: 27651001, 27652001

Oils: Extra Virgin Olive, Virgin Olive, Pure Olive, Pomace Olive.

Pastas: Spaghetti, Fussili, Fettuccine, Lasagna, Penne, Bucatini, Cannelloni, Cappelletti, Macaroni, Mafalde, Vermicelli, Gnocchi, Linguine.

Sauces: Espagnole, Velouté, Béchamel, Hollandaise, Vinaigrette, Albert, Alfredo, Allemande, Aurore, Barbecue, Bernaise, Bercy, Bigarade, Bordelaise, Brown, Chasseur, Choron, Cocktail, Colbert, Cranberry, Crème Anglaise, Diable, Figaro, Genevoise, Hard, Harissa, Hoisin, Louis, Lyonnaise, Maltaise, Marguery, Marinara, Melba, Mornay, Newburg, Normande, Oyster, Parisienne, Piquante, Plum, Puttanesca, Ranchero, Rémoulade, Romesco, Rouille, Shrims, Sofrito, Tabasco, Verte, Worcestershire, White.

Syrups: Grain, Birch, Maple, Flower (Rose/Black/Locust), Berry, Corn, Palm/Date, Golden, Black Treacle, Dark, Molasses, Fruit.

Herbs: Angelica, Basil, Bay, Chervil, Chives, Dill, Fennel, Lemongrass, Marjoram, Oregano, Mint, Parsley, Rosemary, Sage, Tarragon.

Miscellaneous Products: Vinegar: Ital Doro (Italy), Salad Dressing: Remai's (Holland), Mexican Sauce (Casa Fiesta), Olive, Prune.

The Oberoi Patisserie and Delicatessen

10am to 8pm

The Oberoi, Dr Zakir Hussain Marg, New Delhi, Ph: 24363030, 24304071, 24304353

Cheese: Camembert, Cheddar, Colby, Wellington, Stilton, Feta, Gorgonzola, Emmental, Gouda, Edam, Gruye're, Havarti, Limburger, Mascarpone, Swiss, Ricotta, Roquefort.

Oils: Extra Virgin Olive, Virgin Olive, Pure Olive Oil.

Pastas: Spaghetti, Fusilli, Fettuccine, Lasagne, Penne, Bucatini, Cannelloni, Cappelletti, Macaroni, Mafalde, Vermicelli, Ravioli, 17 varieties of Arnesi Pasta (Khuskhus, Polenta).

Vinegar: Ace to Balsamico, De'Modena.

Meat Products: Ham Salami, Italian Salami, Bacon, Smoked Kassler, Chicken Liver Spread, Lamb, Pork Sausage, Tenderloin, German Sausage, English Sausage, British Banger.

Sea Food: Seafood Lyonner, Duck, Smoked Salmon, Salmon Stick.

Miscellaneous Products: Honey (Lemon, Timour), Cereal (Super Cranberry, Dorset).

The Taste

9.30am to 10pm

33, Defence Colony Market, New Delhi,
Ph: 24333733/ 900, 24331900

Oils: Argan, Avocado, Canola, Rapeseed, Flax Seed, Hemp Seed, Macadamia, Palm Kernel, Rice Bran, Safflower, Tea Oil, Walnut, Watermelon, Dill Seed, Rosemary, Tarragon, Thyme, Extra Virgin Olive, Virgin Olive, Pure Olive, Pomace Olive, Corn.

Food Additives: Preservatives, Colour Additives, Flavour Enhancers, Sweeteners, Thickeners, Colour Fixatives.

Pastas: Spaghetti, Fusilli, Fettuccine, Lasagna, Penne, Bucatini, Cannelloni, Cappelletti, Macaroni, Mafalde, Vermicelli, Gnocchi, Linguine, Tubetti, Ravioli.

Noodles: Rice, Vermicelli, Fettuccine, Udon.

Fruits: Strawberry Tree, Sea Grape, American Mayapple, Queen Pineapple, Babacos, Blackberry, Blackcurrant, Blueberry, Carambola, Cranberry, Curuba, Dragon Fruit, Pithaya, Durian, Feijoas, Fig, Gooseberry, Grape Fruit, Grenadilla, Kaffir Lime, Kiwifruit, Kumquat, Longan, Mangosteen, Passion Fruit, Pomelo, Persimmon, Redcurrant, Raspberries, Rambutan, Ugli fruit, Thai Litchi, Peach, Tamarind, Plum

Vegetables: Broccoli, Brussels Sprout, Chinese Broccoli, Oriental mustard, Malabar Gourd, Drumstick, Lolo Rosso, Frisse, Asparagus, Avocado, Celery, Artichoke, Cherry tomatoes,Sweet Corn, Zucchini, Snow Pea, Peppers, Radicchio, Leek, Fennel, Chinese Cabbage, Pok-Choi, Chicory.

Sauces: Espagnole , Velouté, Béchamel, Vinaigrette, Albert, Alfredo, Allemande, Aurore, Barbecue, Bernaise, Bercy, Bigarade, Bordelaise, Brown, Chasseur, Choron, Cocktail, Colbert, Cranberry, Crème Anglaise, Diable, Figaro, Genevoise, Hard, Harissa, Hoisin, Louis, Lyonnaise, Marguery, Marinara, Melba, Mornay, Newburg, Normande, Oyster, Parisienne, Piquante, Plum, Puttanesca, Ranchero, Rémoulade, Romesco, Rouille, Shrims, Sofrito, Tabasco, Verte, Worcestershire, White.

Syrups: Grain, Birch, Maple, Flower (Rose/Black/Locust), Berry, Corn, Palm/Date, Golden, Black Treacle, Dark, Molasses, Fruit.

Herbs: Angelica, Basil, Bay, Chervil, Chives, Dill, Fennel, Lemongrass, Marjoram, Oregano, Mint, Parsley, Rosemary, Sage, Tarragon, Thyme

Sea Food: Prawn, Tiger Jumbo Prawn, King Prawn, Lobster, Squid, Pomfret, Red Snapper, Crab, Shrimp, Octopus, Oyster, Fish, Crab.

Cheese: Camembert, Cheddar, Colby, Wellington, Stilton, Feta, Gorgonzola, Emmental, Gouda, Edam, Gruye're, Havarti, Limburger, Mascarpone, Mozzarella, Parmesan, Romano, Ricotta, Roquefort, Swiss.

Mushroom: Button/White, Chestnut, Chanterelle, Cepes, Oyster, Enokitake, Shiitake, Matsutake, Truffle (White/Black), Morel, Paddy/Straw.

Miscellaneous Products: Mexican Food Items: Refined Beans, Chilli Beans, Pinto Beans, Garbenzo, Fajitas, Enchiladas, Tacos.

Meat Products : Duck, Turkey, Peking Duck, Pork, Bacon, Japanese Quail, Pancetta, Ham, Salami, Sausage, Frankfurter, Muscovy Duck.

True Spices

8am to 9pm

■ **1131, Kucha Harjasval Bazar, Sitaram, Delhi, Ph: 32585931, 9873156081**

Oils: Canola/Rapeseed, Macadamia, Rice Bran, Safflower, Watermelon, Dill Seed, Rosemary, Tarragon, Thyme, Extra Virgin Olive, Virgin Olive, Pure Olive, Pomace Olive, Corn

Pastas: Spaghetti, Fusilli, Fettuccine, Lasagne, Penne, Bucatini, Cannelloni, Cappelletti, Macaroni, Mafalde, Vermicelli, Gnocchi, Linguine, Tubetti, Ravioli.

Noodles: Rice, Vermicelli, Udon, Glass, Spaghetti, Phad-Thai.

Sauces: Barbecue, Brown, Cocktail, Colbert, Crème Anglaise, Harissa, Hoisin, Marinara, Oyster, Plum, Shrimp, Tabasco, Verte, Worcestershire.

Syrups: Grain, Birch, Maple, Flower (Rose/Black/Locust), Berry, Corn, Palm/Date, Golden, Black Treacle, Dark, Molasses, Fruit.

Herbs: Angelica, Basil, Bay, Chervil, Chives, Dill, Fennel, Lemongrass, Marjoram, Oregano, Mint, Parsley, Rosemary, Sage, Tarragon, Thyme.

Sea Food (Tinned): Tuna, Mackerel.

Cheese: Camembert, Cheddar, Colby, Wellington, Stilton, Feta, Gorgonzola, Emmental, Gouda, Edam, Gruye're, Havarti, Limburger, Mascarpone, Mozzarella, Parmesan, Romano, Ricotta, Roquefort, Swiss

Mushroom: Button/White, Chanterelle, Oyster, Shiitake, Matsutake, Morel.

Flour: Arrowroot, Buckwheat, Chickpea, Maize Meal, Semolina.

Twenty Four Seven

24 hours

■ **M 63, Greater Kailash II, New Delhi, Ph: 41435511**

■ **A 1, Lajpat Nagar II, New Delhi, Ph: 41721122, 41721133**

■ **6, Community Center, Saket (PVR Complex), New Delhi, Ph: 41671212**

■ **14-15, Satyam Cineplex, District Centre, Nehru Place, New Delhi, Ph: 26466066**

Oils: Argan, Avocado, Canola/Rapeseed, Flax Seed, Hemp Seed, Macadamia, Palm Kernel, Rice Bran, Safflower, Tea, Lime, Walnut, Watermelon, Extra Virgin Olive, Virgin Olive, Pure Olive, Pomaceve, Corn.

Food Additives: Preservatives, Colour Additives, Flavour Enhancers, Acidity Regulators.

Pastas: Spaghetti, Fusilli, Fettuccine, Lasagne, Penne, Bucatini, Cannelloni, Cappelletti, Macaroni, Mafalde, Vermicelli, Gnocchi, Linguine, Tubetti, Ravioli.

Noodles: Rice, Vermicelli, Fettuccine, Udon, Glass, Spaghetti, Phad-Thai.

Fruits: Strawberry Tree, Sea Grape, American Mayapple, Tamarind, Plum.

Vegetables: Broccoli, Brussels Sprout, Chinese Broccoli, Oriental Mustard, Malabar Gourd, Drumstick, Cherry Tomato, Sweet Corn, Pepper, Chinese Cabbage.

Sauces: Espagnole, Velouté,

Béchamel, Vinaigrette, Albert, Alfredo, Allemande, Aurore, Barbecue, Bernaise, Bercy, Bigarade, Bordelaise, Brown, Chasseur, Choron, Cocktail, Colbert, Cranberry, Crème Anglaise, Diable, Figaro, Genevoise, Hard, Harissa, Hoisin, Louis, Lyonnaise, Maltaise, Marguery, Marinara, Melba, Mornay, Newburg, Normande, Oyster, Parisienne, Piquante, Plum, Puttanesca, Ranchero, Rémoulade, Romesco, Rouille, Shrimp, Sofrito, Tabasco, Verte, Worcestershire.

Syrups: Grain, Birch, Maple, Flower (Rose/Black/Locust), Fruit.

Herbs: Angelica, Basil, Chives, Dill, Fennel, Parsley, Rosemary, Sage.

Sea Food: Prawn, Tiger Jumbo Prawn, King Prawn, Shrimp, Oyster, Crabs, Ham.

Cheese: Camembert, Cheddar, Colby, Wellington, Stilton, Feta, Gorgonzola, Emmental, Gouda, Edam, Mozzarella.

Umesh International

AC
11am to 6pm

304, Khari Bawli, Tilak Bazar, New Delhi

Herbs: Angelica, Basil, Bay, Chervil, Chives, Dill, Fennel, Lemongrass, Marjoram, Oregano, Mint, Parsley, Rosemary, Sage, Tarragon, Thyme.

Miscellaneous Products: (Spices) Cloves, Cassia, Cinnamon, Nutmeg, Mace, Long Pepper, Cumin, Black/White Pepper, Coriander, Turmeric, Fennel.

V K Enterprices

9am to 9pm

131, INA Market, New Delhi, Ph: 9811110186, 24601302

Oils: Argan, Avocado, Canola/Rapeseed, Flax Seed, Hemp Seed, Macadamia, Palm Kernel, Rice Bran, Safflower, Tea, Walnut, Watermelon, Dill Seed, Rosemary, Tarragon, Thyme, Extra Virgin Olive, Virgin Olive, Pure Olive, Pomace Olive, Corn.

Pastas: Fusilli, Lasagne, Penne, Bucatini, Cannelloni, Cappelletti, Macaroni, Mafalde, Vermicelli, Gnocchi, Linguine, Tubetti, Ravioli.

Sauces: Barbecue, Cocktail, Oyster, Plum Sauce.

Syrups: Grain, Birch, Maple, Flower (Rose/Black/Locust), Berry, Corn, Palm/Date, Golden, Black Treacle, Dark, Molasses, Fruit.

Herbs: Angelica, Basil, Bay, Chervil, Chives, Dill, Fennel, Lemongrass, Marjoram, Oregano, Mint, Parsley, Rosemary, Sage, Tarragon, Thyme.

Mushroom: Button/White , Chestnut, Oyster, Shiitake, Matsutake, Morel.

V N Agencies

AC SS
10am to 7pm

G 3/12, 1st Floor, Malviya Nagar, New Delhi, Ph: 9811752771, 46074103, 02

Oils: Extra Virgin Olive, Virgin Olive, Pure Olive, Pomace Olive.

Noodles: Thai Noodles—Phad-Thai.

Sauces: Hollandaise, Alfredo, Aurore, Barbecue, Cocktail, Oyster, Plum, Tabasco, Worcestershire, Black Bean Garlic Sauce.

Syrups: Grain, Birch, Maple,

Flower (Rose/Black/ Locust), Berry, Corn, Palm/Date, Golden, Black Treacle, Dark, Molasses, Bar, Fruit.

Herbs: Angelica, Basil, Bay, Chervil, Chives, Dill, Fennel, Lemongrass, Marjoram, Oregano, Mint, Rosemary, Sage, Tarragon, Thyme.

Sea Food: Prawns, Crabs, Oyster, Tuna Fish.

Cheese: Camembert, Cheddar, Colby, Wellington, Stilton, Feta, Gorgonzola, Emmental, Gouda, Edam, Gruye're, Havarti, Limburger, Mascarpone, Mozzarella, Parmesan, Romano, Ricotta, Roquefort, Swiss.

Mushroom: Button, Chestnut, Oyster, Enokitake, Shiitake, Matsutake.

Miscellaneous Products: Around 15 types of Ragu Sauces, Italian (Arborio rice). 32 different kinds of Thai sauces.

5 Star

10am to 6pm

IV 1/47, Gopi Nath Bazar, Delhi Cantt., Delhi, Ph: 25692428, 9891153299

Oils: Argan, Avocado, Canola/Rapeseed, Flax Seed, Hemp Seed, Macadamia, Palm Kernel, Rice Bran, Safflower, Tea, Lime, Walnut, Watermelon, Dill Seed, Rosemary, Tarragon, Thyme, Extra Virgin Olive, Virgin Olive, Pure Olive, Pomace, Corn.

Food Additives: Preservatives, Colour Addictives, Flavour Enhancers, Emulsifiers, Stabilisers, Binders, Texturisers, Firming Agents, Dough Stergtheners, Conditioners, Sweeteners, Acidity Regulators, Leavening Agents, Anti-Caking Agents, Humectants, Thickeners, Colour Fixatives.

Pastas: Spaghetti, Fusilli, Fettuccine, Lasagne, Penne, Bucatini, Cannelloni, Cappelletti, Macaroni, Mafalde, Vermicelli, Gnocchi, Linguine, Tubetti, Ravioli.

Noodles: Rice, Vermicelli, Fettuccine.

Sauces: Alfredo, Barbecue, Brown, Cocktail, Colbert, Cranberry, Crème Anglaise, Figaro, Hard, Hoisin, Oyster, Plum, Romesco, Shrimp, Tabasco, Worcestershire, White.

Syrups: Grain, Birch, Maple, Berry, Corn, Palm/Date, Golden, Black Treacle, Dark, Molasses, Fruit.

Herbs: Angelica, Basil, Bay, Chervil, Chives, Dill, Fennel, Lemongrass, Marjoram, Oregano, Mint, Parsley, Rosemary, Sage, Tarragon, Thyme.

Sea Food (Canned): Prawn, Crab, Shrimp, Octopus, Oyster, Fish.

Mushrooms: Button/White, Chestnut, Chanterelle, Oyster, Enokitake, Shiitake, Morel.

Miscellaneous Products: All South Indian spices and papads and Gujarati, Maharastrian and South Indian pickles.

CHOCOLATES — ALPHABETICAL

CHOCOLATES — AREA-WISE

HOME CATERERS — ALPHABETICAL

HOME CATERERS — AREA-WISE

HOME CATERERS — CUISINE-WISE

PROFESSIONAL HOME CATERERS — ALPHABETICAL

PROFESSIONAL HOME CATERERS — AREA-WISE

PROFESSIONAL HOME CATERERS — CUISINE-WISE

TIFFIN SERVICES — ALPHABETICAL

TIFFIN SERVICES — AREA-WISE

COOKING CLASSES — ALPHABETICAL

COOKING CLASSES — AREA-WISE

COOKING CLASSES — CUISINE-WISE

FOOD SHOPS — ALPHABETICAL

FOOD SHOPS — AREA-WISE

FOOD SHOPS — CATEGORY-WISE

CAVIAR

Caspian Caviar & Fine Food...75

CHEESE

Allied Fruits & Florists...70
Amrit...71
Anand...71
Bhutani....72
Big Apple...73
Dairy Craft India...76
Dee's Chawla Store...76
Defence Store...77
Flanders Dairy...79
Food Max...79
Garg Dastak...80
Gogia's...80
Harmilapi...81
Inder...83
Indian Dairy...84
Jainsons...84
Lakshmi...85
Le Marche...86
Lucky...87
Malik...88
Modern Bazar...89
Morning Store...89
Morning Store...90
New Anand...90
Om The Super Market...90
Pioneer...92
Rahul...93
Rajasthan...93
S K Store...94
Sharda...96
Shri Morning Palace...97
Shri Sant Lal Ramji Dass...97
Star Bazaar...98
Steak House...99
Store 18 Noida...99
Oberoi Patisserie and Delicatessen, The...100
The Taste...101
Truspices...102
Twenty Four Seven...102
V N Agencies...103

FLOUR

A.T. Exims...69
Agrim Sales...69
Amrit...71
Anand...71
Dee's Chawla Store...76
Defence Store...77
Holy Land...82
Jainsons...84
Lakshmi...85
Le Marche...86
Lucky...87
Morning Store...89
Morning Store...90
Palkit Impex...91
Rajasthan...93
Shri Morning Palace...97
Steak House...99
Truspices...102

FOOD ADDITIVES

5 Star...104
A.T. Exims...69
Agrim Sales...69
Anand...71
Bhutani....72
Big Apple...73
Dee's Chawla Store...76
Defence Store...77
Garg Dastak...80
Gogia's...80
Harmilapi...81
Jainsons...84
Lakshmi...85
Modern Bazar...89
Morning Store...89
Om The Super Market...90
Rahul...93
Shri Morning Palace...97
Shri Sant Lal Ramji Dass...97
Star Bazaar...98
Steak House...99
Store 18 Noida...99
The Taste...101
Twenty Four Seven...102

FRUITS

Ahuja Vegetable Store...69
Allied Fruits & Florists...70
Big Apple...73
Dee's Chawla Store...76
Ever Green Veg & Fruit...78
First Bite Fruit & Vegetables...79
Gogia's...80
Green Vegetable Mart...81
Holy Land...82
Jainsons...84
KLG Imports and Exports...85
Le Marche...86
Modern Bazar...89
Morning Store...89
Morning Store...90
Pindi Fruit Mart...92
S Naresh Kumar...94
Sabji Kendra...95
Sachdeva Vegetable and Fruits...95
Sethi Fruits and Vegetable...96
Sharda...96
Shiv Fruit Mart...97
The Taste...101
Twenty Four Seven...102

HERBS

5 Star...104
Agrim Sales...69
Ahuja Vegetable Store...69
Allied Fruits & Florists...70
Amrit...71
Anand...71
Big Apple...73
Dee's Chawla Store...76
Defence Store...77
Dera Farms...77
Food Max...79
French Farms...80
Garg Dastak...80
Gogia's...80
Harmilapi...81
Holy Land...82
IFB Agro...83
Inder...83
Jainsons...84
Lakshmi...85
Le Marche...86
Lucky...87
Malik...88
Modern Bazar...89
Morning Store...89
Morning Store...90
Navdanya...90
New Anand...90
Om The Super Market...90
Pindi Fruit Mart...92
Rahul...93
Rajasthan...93
S K Store...94
S Naresh Kumar...94
Sachdeva Vegetable and Fruits...95
Sethi Fruits and Vegetable...96
Sharda...96
Shri Morning Palace...97
Shri Sant Lal Ramji Dass...97
Star Bazaar...98
Steak House...99
Store 18 Noida...99
Suresh Kumar...100
The Taste...101
Truspices...102
Twenty Four Seven...102
Umesh International...103
V K Enterprices...103
V N Agencies...103

MEAT PRODUCT

Ajit Farms...70
Allied Fruits & Florists...70
Amrit...71
Anand...71
Caspian Caviar & Fine Food...75
Ceegate Overseas...75
Chicken Ette...75
Dairy Craft India...76
Debon Meat Shop...76
Defence Store...77
French Farms...80
Green Chic Chop...81
Harmilapi...81
Holy Land...82
Inder...83
Jainsons...84
Khub Chand...85
Lakshmi...85
Le Marche...86
Lucky...87
Modern Bazar...89
Morning Store...89
Palkit Impex...91

PASTES

SAUCES

SEA FOOD

SEA WEED

SYRUPS

VEGETABLE

VINEGAR

NOTES

ABOUT THE AUTHOR

Marryam H Reshii has been a food critic and gastronomy writer for over a decade. During this period she has tasted diverse culinary traditions from India as well as across the globe. This has given her an insight into the cuisines spanning cultures and traditions as well as into the latest trends in food. For someone who has visited the entire gamut of eateries in a number of cities, she is as aware of a *bhaji* seller on Chennai's Marina Beach as of Andy Yau's latest temple of gastronomy in London. In her column in *What's Hot,* a *Times of India* publication, the acclaimed food writer maps the city's latest eating joints with alacrity. Undoubtedly, one can say she knows Delhi's eating places like the back of her hand. Be it the most cutting-edge five-star restaurant, a medium-range eatery or even a *dhaba*, she can tell you its USP.

She is working on a book on food and occasionally contributes to a number of leading publications on travel also. Among her many interests she is hugely passionate about forests and avian fauna. Marryam has written two books — *Kashmir: The Himalayan Paradise* and *Kashmir: The Mystery*, and is also involved with the documenting of the long-forgotten recipes of Kashmiri cuisine. In addition, she has just completed *Eating Out in India: 101 Favourite Restaurants,* published by Times Group Books. This book covers the most popular restaurants all over the country and includes such obscure locations as Madurai, Indore and Dharamshala. She travels extensively and is fond of picking up ingredients from around the world.